John Michael Lerma's

 GARDEN COUNTY

Where Everyone Is Welcome to Sit at the Table

Sharon gave me this book July, 2006
The Author has been to the resort -
Very nice

JOHN MICHAEL LERMA'S

Garden County

WHERE EVERYONE IS WELCOME TO SIT AT THE TABLE

For Dale -
May all your gatherings
be joyous.
I hope you love my
recipes.

SYREN BOOK COMPANY
MINNEAPOLIS

Most Syren Books are available at special quantity discounts for bulk purchases for sales promotions, premiums, fund-raising, and educational needs. For details, write

Syren Book Company
Special Sales Department
5120 Cedar Lake Road
Minneapolis, MN 55416

Published by
Syren Book Company
5120 Cedar Lake Road
Minneapolis, MN 55416

Printed in the United States of America on acid-free paper

ISBN-13: 978-0-929636-50-4
ISBN-10: 0-929636-50-3

LCCN 2005927908

Cover design by Kyle G. Hunter
Book design by Wendy Holdman
Cover photography by Lanee' Benson, photographer, and Jennifer Frederick Terrell, photographer's assistant

To order additional copies of this book see the form
at the back of this book or go to www.itascabooks.com

Contents

*This book is for Thelma Anderson,
a joyous cook, gardener, and grandmother.*

*And for Elaine Strand (Grand Forks, North Dakota Public
Library), who convinced me when I was young and had no
direction to return to school and obtain my diploma.*

These two women changed my life in so many wonderful ways.

John Michael Lerma's

GARDEN COUNTY

Where Everyone Is Welcome to Sit at the Table

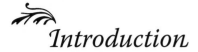

Introduction

*G*ARDEN COUNTY: where everyone is welcome to sit at the table. In my frame of mind, suitably named Garden County, everyone is welcome.

Nothing says "welcome" more than an invitation to sit at the table and share food with a community of friends, neighbors, and future friends. Instantly the conversation will begin. Perhaps it may be a comment about the food that has been prepared, or a comment on the weather, but kinship begins with that first word and the first crust of bread that is broken.

Garden County is an actual location. It is my and Chad's backyard. Disenchanted by the corporate world's daily demands and increasingly repulsive world news events, I dug up half of my backyard and planted flowers, vegetables, berries, and shrubs. Eventually, I found a small block of wood behind the raspberry canes where I would sit and watch bees, by the thousands, diligently working to extract pollen and pollinate the raspberry canes. I found my day-to-day problems draining down into the ground, where they were composted so to speak. I felt at peace and calmed by the activity that was occurring in my garden. Naturally, I came to call this sitting area my contemplation seat. Ultimately, Garden County built itself. In a ten-foot-by-ten-foot plot of land between two garages in the Highland Park district of Saint Paul, Minnesota, "the Back Forty" was christened; Fairy Crossing, Sunflower Territory, Strawberry Piazza, Concord Grape Way, and many other designations came into existence. Some paths or areas have signage; others are made known only by Chad's or my pointing and explaining to amused guests that this is "the Back Forty."

Out of our garden came produce. Having been raised on a farm in the Red River Valley of North Dakota, I knew what to do with the rewards of our land. I had the knowledge of canning berries, vegetables, and fruits passed on to me by my grandmother Thelma Anderson. I was taught to freeze foods that couldn't be canned. Most important, I learned how to cook with what was available during certain seasons of the year. Nothing went to waste. These skills returned as our little plot of land rejoiced in being tilled again. Our house, built in 1914, had originally been a farm sitting atop a hill high above the Mississippi River.

Chad and I soon began hosting gatherings in our little house for our friends, neighbors, and their friends. We have always adopted the attitude of "the more the merrier." A friend would call to explain that they had visitors from out of town, and we would always tell them to bring them along. Before long those out-of-towners felt as if they had lived in our community of friends for years. Due to these gatherings, recipes began to resurface as I scanned notebooks in which my grandmother had written her recipes. When I returned to the Red River Valley for a visit, I would page through stacks of recipes books written by generations of relatives, some only listing the ingredients—no measurements, no oven temperatures, and no cooking times. I remember a good many of these recipes from years of making them alongside my grandmother, so I am now able to duplicate and prepare them, adding necessary information to the recipes.

The entire progression of our garden was such a wonderfully natural process. It was as if the former farmyard was gladdened by our presence. It was happy to have its land turned and tended to again. One of my greatest garden accomplishments was to grow corn in a ten-foot-by-ten-foot plot of land for two years. When the ears were ready, Chad or I would pick what we needed for that meal and prepare it. Our guests would comment on the color and sweetness of the corn. Originally, Chad stated that there was no way I could grow corn in Highland Park. That statement motivated me even more. I knew I had to be successful. I was very proud of what I could produce with a small plot of land, some seeds, and a little weeding. In the fall, I gathered the corn stalks, tied them together, and created a harvest scene in the front yard for Halloween and Thanksgiving. All for the price of a handful of seeds.

This book, then, is the next step in Garden County: recovering the satisfaction of gardening, cooking, and entertaining in one's life. It has assisted me in making a distraught world a healthier space to continue living in. On my way to work, I would stop and smell a rose or cut it and bring it along to my office. I would grab a handful of raspberries from the canes to bring along for the drive. When I arrived home, weary from hard work, I would instantly be greeted by ferocious-colored flowers, rabbits hopping down the garden paths, squirrels running amok, the call of a cardinal, and total tranquillity. My mind would switch from my current job to what I could prepare for our supper or whether we should call friends to come join us. That is why I wanted to share these recipes and anecdotes with you. Create your own Garden County, even if the only soil you can till is in a clay pot on your front steps.

The recipes in this book call for many homemade ingredients such as relish, pizza dough, and breads. I have the time to prepare the dough and let it rise. Ultimately, with time at a premium for all of us, homemade can be accomplished during weekends or days off. Try not to plan too much—just one or two recipes. Once you become proficient at them, you will find the time to add more homemade recipes to your repertoire. I have been canning and preparing homemade foods since I was a child. I've learned how to set bread dough and run errands while it is rising. That doesn't mean you can't simply use a ready-made ingredient to follow these recipes. I encourage doing that if it will make your life easier and you decide to share my food ideas at your gatherings. I only suggest preparing everything from scratch because I've done it that way all my life.

This book is about gathering. If the gathering becomes a chore or too much work, it is not worth it. Go ahead and use commercially prepared items, but enjoy the gathering and your guests. If you take anything away with you from this book, it is this message: It's not the food you prepare or the drinks or the decor of your home. It's the gathering of the people that you'll remember tomorrow—the laughter and the conversation.

Please note that many of my recipes call for alternate ingredients, for example, regular, low-fat, or fat-free. This means that I have tested these recipes with each of those ingredients. It also means that the taste is not affected; otherwise, I wouldn't recommend the transition from "full fat" to fat-free. I have created a variety of recipes for my family because Chad, Heather (our daughter), and I prefer a low-fat diet. We're active and love to bike, walk, travel, garden, and live. I formerly weighed 338 pounds, but that is another book. I have lost more than 110 pounds recently and continue to lose weight and stay in shape, with exercise, activity, and the support of Weight Watchers, my friends, and family.

I preach the message of gardening, gathering, and cooking. Create fabulous gatherings by adopting a policy of no politics, work-related topics, religion, or bad news conversations. Talk instead about your children, your partner, your travels, and your goals. Invite conversations by asking questions, pouring another glass of wine, or offering to share a piece of cheesecake with the person you're sitting next to. Some of the best conversations can come from the guests of guests. I absolutely adore it when my gatherings include future friends. When I lived in Grand Forks, North Dakota, I hosted "Orphan" dinners at Thanksgiving, Christmas Eve, and Easter. I would contact our local air force base and invite service personnel to join us who had no family nearby. The other guests at my gathering were friends, neighbors, and their friends who had no families to join. Some of my finest memories are of those dinners. It is touching to see someone who would be alone smile, laugh, and not notice they are far away from home during that holiday. Such is the mind-set of Garden County.

I hope you enjoy my suggestions for menu planning and your gatherings. I suggest adopting an Italian frame of mind with regard to cooking. Italians do not associate guilt with food. They take their time in eating and afterward walk arm in arm for hours, chatting. It's really quite beautiful and one of the reasons I will return to Italy again and again. Don't judge your neighbors but invite them to your next gathering and embark on inventing your own serene frame of mind in your Garden County.

The Academy Awards Gathering

*T*HIS CELEBRATION GATHERING started back in 1973, when movies began to shape my hopes, dreams, and, admittedly, some nightmares about life. At the age of twelve, I saw *The Poseidon Adventure* fifteen times during its first run at the Plaza Twin Theater located next to K-Mart in Grand Forks. Until that time, I didn't take movies too seriously. I spent Saturdays with my sister at *Puss-in-Boots, HR Pufnstuf,* and a weird parable about nature striking back called *Frogs.* Something was happening to me in 1973, besides puberty. After becoming obsessed with *The Poseidon Adventure,* I walked a couple of blocks to the Cinema International. This incredibly large-screen movie theater was somewhat off-limits because they showed movies like *2001: A Space Odyssey, Camelot,* and other films that were being shown in a format called "subscription." (You were required to purchase a subscription for movies being released the following season.) I didn't need a subscription ticket for *Pufnstuf.* My mom said they built the Cinema International for people "who had money." I guess the Plaza Twin Theater was built for us fifty-cent-ticket types. Once I found that subscription tickets were no longer needed at the Cinema International, I beheld riches such as *Cabaret, Paper Moon, The Way We Were,* and *The Exorcist.* I didn't realize it, but by leaving the little twin theater next to K-Mart, Witchie-poo was being replaced by something much more evil and controversial. It was a new world. It may not have been as psychedelic as *Living Island,* but it was just as colorful.

In early spring, while working on my fingering during piano practice, I noticed the *ABC Evening News* announcing the Oscar nominations. I felt the announcement held something exciting, so I listened carefully, writing down the major nominees in my piano practice book. The year before, I had walked into the living room and joined Mom in watching an awards ceremony. The nominees for best actress were being read and short scenes from their movies were shown. I was really impressed by the scene from *Cabaret.* Then Liza Minnelli was named best actress of the year. Mom was talking behind me. I really didn't understand what she was telling me about Marlon Brando winning for best actor and a Native American woman accepting his award. I hadn't watched an awards show up to that point in my life, so I thought that Native Americans accepting someone's award was normal. The following year there was much more excitement because *The Exorcist* had been nominated for ten Academy Awards. There was real electricity in the air that year, and a ritual began that has lasted more than thirty years.

It began as I typed up an Oscar ballot and handed it out in my seventh-grade music class. After class, I tallied the ballots and posted the winners for best picture, actor, actress, and song by the door of the music room. I remember *The Exorcist* being chosen as best picture. However, most of us were thirteen years old and were unable to see the movie without a parent or guardian. I went with a family friend and was disappointed when I didn't faint or become ill as I watched the demon-possessed little girl. I wanted to be a part of all the excitement that was associated with films. I wanted to be a part of the "happening," the gathering of movie-goers and their experience.

So, what does this have to do with celebration and cooking? Because of my longing to be a part of the moviegoers' experience, the Academy Awards held an extraordinary quality for me. It was a gathering that I wanted to belong to or be invited to. It was obvious in my teenage dreamer's mind that I would be invited someday. I would be nominated. It didn't matter for what; I would be nominated for something, I thought. That first Oscar ballot, in seventh-grade music class, led to a yearly ballot that I handed out to the entire school and was typed on carbon copy paper that stained my hands purple. It led to rushing to Piggly Wiggly on the way home from school to purchase special treats to enjoy while watching the Oscar telecast, and finally, my annual Academy Award parties after I moved into my own apartment and, recently, my own home.

My favorite Academy Awards gathering was in 1987, the year Michael Douglas was named best actor for *Wall Street.* Best picture was *The Last*

Emperor, and Cher won best actress for *Moonstruck.* I covered my dining room table with crab salad, assorted crackers, canned mandarin oranges, pineapple, and peaches. My best stoneware plates held deli meats, assorted cheeses, and buns. The centerpiece was a sheet cake in the shape of "Oscar" decorated in bright gold buttercream frosting. Everyone was greeted as they walked up to the door (we didn't have a red carpet) by one of my friends (the paparazzi), who took their photo with my old Polaroid instant camera. Once the Polaroid photos developed, they were pinned to a bulletin board in the dining room for all my guests to see. Ballots were handed out before the telecast, and everyone picked their favorites. One dollar was collected from each guest and placed in an envelope as a prize. At the end of the evening, all the ballots were tallied to see who guessed the most winners; that person was presented with the envelope filled with the dollar bills. During the commercials, everyone laughed, gossiped, and had wonderful conversations. The evening was a hit as the food disappeared and champagne flowed.

Each year, I try to serve exciting but comfortable foods that everyone will enjoy. Themes such as "Deli," "Seafood," "Roasted," and "Spring" come to mind when I think back to the buffets I have served at my annual gatherings. One thing to bear in mind is to keep it simple. One year, I chose the theme "Dynasty" fashioned after the hit television show. Trying to keep up with the Carringtons, and serving strawberries from Chile the way Alexis liked them, was a daunting task at best but also unrealistic unless I had a staff and a good deal of funds. As a host, I didn't want to continue cooking once my guests arrived or serve foods while the show was taking place. I wanted to be a part of the "happening," part of the gathering, and part of the laughter, not slaving in the kitchen and observing my party from another room. The solution: prepare ahead of time; plan and create a list. Also, at the end of the evening, refrigerate what you can save and maybe rinse a couple of dishes, but simply sit back, finish the remaining champagne, and watch the Oscar after-parties on television. You can always clean up the next day. As a good planner, you can request the next day off from work. I always ask at least six months in advance for the day off after the Academy Awards. You can always practice your acceptance speech while washing the dishes and cleaning up after your Academy Award gathering guests. "And the winner is . . ."

SUGGESTED LIST OF OPTIONS

- Champagne Slurry with frozen fruit and berries (strawberries, peaches, pineapple, melon, and grapes)
- Crab Salad
- Golden Statue Celebration Cake
- Gourmet Pizzas
    - Margherita
    - Garden-Fresh Pesto
    - Salmon Asparagus with Balsamic Vinegar
    - Herbed Shrimp
- Nuclear Long Island Teas
- Marinated Olives
- Pesto Cheese Ball with Sun-Dried Tomatoes
- Salmon
    - Salmon Spread
    - Whiskey-Soaked Salmon
    - Salmon Loaf
    - Cool Smoked Salmon Pizza
- Supreme Chocolate Cake
- Tortilla Garlic Swirls
- Warm Spinach Dip

⸕ Champagne Slurry with Frozen Fruits and Berries

The name "Slurry" came about a couple of years ago when I made this drink for several guests at a backyard barbecue. I had a large glass barrel jug that I use for making Raspberry Cordial in the winter. I added the ingredients and placed a ladle by the jar for my guests to serve themselves. One guest enjoyed eating only the champagne-marinated fruit. After one large glass of "pickled" fruit, she began slurring her words when she spoke. Thus began the name "Slurry." So enjoy in moderation and speak softly.

> Two (750 ml) bottles of good-quality, but inexpensive, dry champagne.
> Approximately three pounds of mixed frozen fruit (peaches, pineapple, grapes, melon, and strawberries) and/or berries (raspberries, blueberries, golden berries, and strawberries). Be creative with your combinations.

1. Place frozen fruit and/or berries in a punch bowl, decorative large container, or pitchers.
2. Pour champagne over frozen fruit/berries. Let stand 1 to 2 hours as fruit/berries will thaw and chill champagne. Serve in glasses garnished with fresh mint.

❡ Crab Salad

This is a wonderful addition for an Academy Award party because you can use this treat in so many ways. I serve with assorted crackers, on toasted bread squares, or rolled in a low-fat 10-inch flour tortilla, chilled overnight, and sliced into ¼-inch rounds. One of my favorite applications is to place the prepared crab salad on a toasted pita round and cover it with low-fat shredded mozzarella cheese. Place this personal pizza under the broiler or in the toast oven until the cheese melts. A great treat for your guests or a guilty pleasure for yourself.

> 12 ounces crab meat, shredded (canned or imitation is fine also)
> ¼ cup Grandma's Sweet Cucumber Relish (see under Festival of the Moonflower)
> 2 tablespoons sweet onion (optional)
> Also optional: add 2 tablespoons chopped black olives and ¼ cup fat-free shredded cheddar cheese.
> ¼ cup good-quality mayonnaise (regular, low-fat, or fat-free)

1. Place crab meat in a medium mixing bowl and blend with relish and onion.
2. Add mayonnaise and combine. Chill in airtight container for 20 minutes to let flavors develop.

Makes approximately two cups of salad.

Golden Statue Celebration Cake

  3 cups cake flour
  ½ teaspoon salt
  1 pound + 1 cup unsalted butter, room temperature, divided
  1 pound sugar
  6 large eggs
  ½ cup buttermilk
  3 teaspoons pure vanilla extract, divided
  1 cup all-vegetable shortening
  1 teaspoon almond extract
  2 pounds (approximately 8 cups) sifted confectioner's sugar
  ¼ cup whipping cream

1. Preheat oven to 325 degrees. Prepare two 9-inch cake pans or one 13- × 9-inch oblong cake pan with cooking spray.
2. Sift together the flour and salt. Set aside.
3. In the bowl of an electric mixer, beat 1 pound butter until creamy with the flat paddle on medium-high speed. Add the pound of sugar gradually and continue to beat until light and fluffy. Add the eggs one at a time, beating well after each addition, scraping down the bowl once or twice with a spatula. Beat in 2 teaspoons vanilla.
4. Add the sifted dry ingredients in three batches, alternating with buttermilk. Combine well after each addition, scraping bowl as needed. After all the dry ingredients are added, beat for about 2 minutes on medium speed to thoroughly combine. Do not overmix.
5. Scrape the batter into the prepared pan, smoothing the top with a spatula. Bake 50 to 60 minutes, or until a toothpick tests clean. The cake should be golden. Cool 10 minutes before gently removing from the pans. Place on a cake board and cool completely before decorating. Oblong cake may be sliced in half and filled with buttercream frosting, jam, or berry curds.
6. In the bowl of an electric mixer, cream the remaining cup of butter at room temperature and 1 cup shortening. Add 1 teaspoon vanilla, 1 teaspoon almond extract, and whipping cream. Mix well. Gradually

add confectioner's sugar, one cup at a time, beating well on medium speed. Scrape sides and bottom of the bowl often with a spatula. Keep icing covered until ready to use.

ASSEMBLY

Have all components ready. Tint 1 cup of icing black and 1 cup gold. Use white icing to fill and frost sides of cake. Smooth sides with an angled spatula or back of a spoon. Fill icing bag with black icing using #3 Wilton tip. You may also use a large envelope and cut a small hole in the corner to create the outline of the Academy Award. Slowly and lightly apply pressure to the icing bag or envelope. Using a photo or computer print-out, begin to create your outline of the award. I also write the event, date, and/or a welcome message to my guests in black icing. Fill icing bag with gold icing using a number #16 Wilton tip. This tip will create puffy rosettes or stars, depending on your preference. You may spoon the gold icing within the outline and smooth with the back of a spoon or angled spatula. I like to add a ruffle around the bottom of the cake and other embellishments appropriate to the occasion. Be creative and design your own award-winning cake for your gathering.

Pizza Margherita

This pizza, which represents the colors of the Italian flag (red, green, and white), comes with a rich history. I learned to make this while in Italy and was told that pizza maker Raffaele Esposito created Pizza Margherita in 1889 as a tribute to the queen of Italy. The Italians believe that a pizza should not be loaded with ingredients and that less is more. This pizza also is called Neapolitan or thin-crust pizza. Make sure you look for the freshest and best-quality ingredients, and you'll produce a pizza your guests will love. I grow my own Sicilian basil and can my own roma tomatoes, so this pizza represents two of my favorite flavors from the garden.

1 12-ounce, room-temperature pizza dough (see Pizza Dough
under The Basics)
1 tablespoon good-quality extra virgin olive oil
1 cup Tuscan Tomato Sauce (see Tuscan Tomato Sauce under The
Basics)
½ pound hand-packed mozzarella cheese, sliced ¼ inch thick
Fresh basil leaves, about 12, washed and dried

1. Preheat oven to 450 degrees. Stretch room-temperature pizza dough
   into a thin round crust and place on a cornmeal-dusted pizza pan,
   parchment paper, or baking sheet. Do not use a rolling pin as this will
   push gases out of dough.
2. Drizzle stretched pizza dough with extra virgin olive oil. Using pastry
   brush, spread oil around dough, including edge. Add tomato sauce
   and spread evenly. Place sliced mozzarella cheese on top of tomato
   sauce. Do not add basil until after pizza comes out of oven.
3. Slide pizza into the hot oven and bake for 15–20 minutes. Baking
   times will depend on thickness of crust and amount of toppings.
4. Transfer to a cutting board and add fresh basil leaves. Brush edge of
   crust with olive oil to add shine and flavor.

Serves six.

⸙ Garden-Fresh Pesto Pizza

  1 12-ounce, room-temperature pizza dough (see Pizza Dough
      under The Basics)
  1 teaspoon good-quality extra virgin olive oil
  ⅔ cup basil pesto (see Basil Pesto under The Basics)
  ½ cup freshly grated Parmigiano-Reggiano cheese
  ¼ cup freshly grated Pecorino Romano cheese
  Fresh basil leaves, about 8, washed and dried

1. Preheat oven to 450 degrees. Stretch room-temperature pizza dough into a thin round crust and place on a cornmeal-dusted pizza pan, parchment paper, or baking sheet. Do not use a rolling pin as this will push gases out of dough.
2. Drizzle stretched pizza dough with extra virgin olive oil. Using pastry brush, spread oil around dough, including edge. Add basil pesto and spread evenly. Grate cheeses over basil pesto. Do not add basil leaves until after pizza comes out of oven.
3. Slide pizza into the hot oven and bake for 10–15 minutes. Baking times will depend on thickness of crust and amount of toppings.
4. Transfer to a cutting board and place fresh basil leaves on top of the baked cheeses. Brush edge of crust with olive oil to add shine and flavor.

Serves six.

ƒ Salmon Asparagus with Balsamic Vinegar Pizza

Start this superb gourmet pizza with the best salmon you can find at your local seafood market. My favorite salmon is wild salmon, which begins swimming up rivers in Alaska toward the end of April and into May on their annual migration through glacial waters. The earliest run is the king salmon in the Copper River.

Copper River salmon, caught after their long swim through cold waters, have a firm texture, extra Omega-3 oil, and plenty of tremendous flavor. A carefully controlled catch keeps wild salmon environmentally sustainable. These fish are available fresh for only about three weeks, and it's worth the extra price to order this fish as a change from the usual pink farm-raised variety.

> 1 12-ounce, room-temperature pizza dough (see Pizza Dough
>   under The Basics)
> 1 tablespoon good-quality extra virgin olive oil
> 6 ounces fresh salmon
> 1 tablespoon good-quality balsamic vinegar
> Kosher or Hawaiian salt
> Freshly ground black pepper
> 8 fresh asparagus stalks cut into ½-inch sections
> ½ cup freshly shredded mozzarella cheese
> ¼ cup freshly grated Pecorino Romano cheese

1. Preheat oven to 450 degrees. Stretch room temperature pizza dough into a thin round crust and place on a cornmeal-dusted pizza pan, parchment paper, or baking sheet. Do not use a rolling pin as this will push gases out of dough.
2. Drizzle stretched pizza dough with extra virgin olive oil. Using pastry brush, spread oil around dough, including edge. Set side.
3. Drizzle a heavy-bottom skillet with olive oil and place salmon, skin side down, in hot oil. Sprinkle with salt and pepper. Spoon balsamic vinegar over salmon and let it soak in during the cooking process. Salmon is done when it changes color and becomes flaky after about

4–6 minutes per side. Peel skin from the filet. Using a fork, break up the salmon filet to distribute on pizza.

4. In a sauté pan over medium-high heat, place asparagus and drizzle with olive oil. Sprinkle with salt and sauté until asparagus turns a bright green color, usually 3–4 minutes. Add 3 tablespoons water to the pan and cover for a minute or two. Remove from heat.

5. Spread cooled salmon and asparagus evenly over oiled pizza dough. Cover with shredded and grated cheeses.

6. Slide pizza into the hot oven and bake for 20–30 minutes. Baking times will depend on thickness of crust and amount of toppings.

7. Transfer to a cutting board. Brush edge of crust with olive oil to add shine and flavor.

Serves six.

⸕ Herbed Shrimp Pizza

    1 12-ounce, room-temperature pizza dough (see Pizza Dough
       under The Basics)
    1 tablespoon good-quality extra virgin olive oil
    6 ounces medium-size shrimp, peeled and deveined with tails off
    Sprinkling of fresh herbs—basil, oregano, English or French thyme,
       and chive
    Kosher or Hawaiian salt and freshly ground black pepper
    ½ cup freshly shredded mozzarella cheese
    ¼ cup freshly grated Pecorino Romano cheese

1. Preheat oven to 450 degrees. Stretch room-temperature pizza dough into a thin round crust and place on a cornmeal-dusted pizza pan, parchment paper, or baking sheet. Do not use a rolling pin as this will push gases out of dough.

2. Drizzle stretched pizza dough with extra virgin olive oil. Using pastry brush, spread oil around dough, including edge. Set side.

3. Drizzle a heavy-bottom skillet with olive oil and add shrimp, herbs, salt, and pepper. Cook over medium heat until shrimp turn pink, about 8–10 minutes. Remove from heat and spread evenly over the pizza dough.
4. Cover the cooked shrimp with shredded and grated cheeses.
5. Slide pizza into the hot oven and bake for 20–30 minutes. Baking times will depend on thickness of crust and amount of toppings.
6. Transfer to a cutting board. Brush edge of crust with olive oil to add shine and flavor.

Serves six.

⸖ Nuclear Long Island Teas

This truly has a nuclear reaction when you add the sugar, so make sure you mix all the ingredients in a container that can control the mushroom cloud of fizz. This recipe can be deceptive, as it is cool and delicious but packs a powerful punch. Make sure to collect everyone's car keys before offering them this potent but pleasurable libation. Add a paper umbrella and slice of fruit to begin the festive mood even before the first sip is taken.

½ cup light rum	¼ cup triple sec
½ cup vodka	Juice of 1 lemon
½ cup gin	¼ cup superfine sugar
½ cup tequila	5½ cups cola-flavored soda

1. In a large stock pot, bowl, or pitcher, combine liquors, lemon juice, and cola. Stir.
2. Slowly add the sugar. You will get a reaction, but stir until mixed.
3. Pour mixture into a decorative 2-quart pitcher and serve with fresh mint rubbed on glass rims.

⸎ Marinated Olives

I like to use a variety of olives that still have pits. This is the ultimate in finger food and goes very well with the Pesto Cheese Ball and the Gourmet Pizzas. You may also use blue cheese–stuffed olives and pimiento-stuffed olives. The combinations are only limited by what is available at your local market.

    1 cup green olives
    1 cup black olives
    1 cup kalamata olives
    1 tablespoon extra virgin olive oil
    1 large garlic clove, minced
    1 tablespoon fresh oregano, chopped
    1 tablespoon fresh English or French thyme, chopped
    1 tablespoon fresh rosemary, chopped
    1 tablespoon freshly squeezed lemon juice
    Freshly grated Pecorino Romano cheese

Mix all ingredients in a large bowl. Let the olives and herbs develop their flavors at least ½ hour before serving. Serve with a dusting of grated Pecorino Romano cheese.

⸎ Pesto Cheese Ball with Sun-dried Tomatoes

    2 8-ounce packages regular, low-fat, or fat-free cream cheese (room
        temperature)
    ¼ cup basil pesto* (see The Basics for recipe or buy a jar at your
        favorite store)
    1 medium jar sun-dried tomatoes, rinsed and drained

1. Mix both packages of softened cream cheese and basil pesto in the bowl of mixer fitted with paddle. You may also blend with your hands as this works better than using a spoon or whisk. This will ensure that the pesto is well blended with cream cheese. Once blended, press into a ball shape and refrigerate until chilled.
2. Once chilled, place pesto cheese ball on a decorative plate lined with Italian parsley or other green leafy herb. Arrange drained sun-dried tomatoes around the cheese ball, creating interesting patterns, or simply cover entire cheese ball.
3. Serve with an assortment of crackers, cracker bread pieces, or home-made pita chips.

*You may use any flavor pesto for this recipe, such as thyme pesto, sage pesto, or oregano pesto to delight your guests.

⨍ Salmon

I adore salmon. Smoked salmon, red salmon, pink salmon, and, most of all, Copper River salmon, which is only available for about three to four weeks out of each year. Serving salmon at your Academy Award gathering is a must. It's an elegant addition to your table and delicious to snack on throughout the entire award show. As with any fish, however, serve it on a bed of ice to keep the dish well chilled for the entire evening (except for the Salmon Loaf, which is served warm)—remember the Academy Awards can last for hours. Food safety is extremely important, since any foodborne germs can endanger your guests as well as your reputation as a host, and that could take a lifetime to live down. Here are a few of my favorite salmon dishes that you may serve with crackers, baked pita chips, and crudités.

Salmon Spread

1 8-ounce package cream cheese, softened (fat-free, low-fat, or
    regular)
½ cup sour cream (fat-free, low-fat, or regular)
1 teaspoon freshly squeezed lemon juice
½ teaspoon Worcestershire sauce
⅛ teaspoon cayenne pepper
1 teaspoon chopped fresh dill weed
½ teaspoon kosher or Hawaiian salt
¼ teaspoon freshly ground black pepper
2 tablespoons chopped green onion
12 ounces smoked salmon, chopped*

1. In an electric mixer, beat the cream cheese with the paddle attachment until smooth.
2. Add sour cream, lemon juice, Worcestershire sauce, cayenne pepper, dill, salt, and black pepper. With mixer on medium, combine.
3. Remove paddle attachment and gently fold in green onion and salmon. Chill at least 1 hour before serving. Place serving container on ice to keep chilled. Serve with crackers and/or crudités.

*If you are unable to find smoked salmon, you may use fresh or canned. Simply add 1 teaspoon liquid smoke.

Whiskey-Soaked Salmon

1 pound fresh smoked salmon, without skin
1 cup good-quality whiskey such as Jack Daniels

Place salmon in a container large enough to hold the entire fillet. Pour the whiskey over the salmon and cover tightly. Refrigerate 6 hours or overnight before serving. Offer to your guests on a wooden cutting board or decorative platter garnished with fresh dill weed or sprinkled with fresh rosemary leaves.

⸕ Salmon Loaf

1 14-ounce can red or pink salmon
2 large eggs
Kosher or Hawaiian salt and freshly ground black pepper
3 teaspoons fresh dill weed, chopped
¼ cup green onions, chopped with green parts
1 sleeve saltine crackers (regular or fat-free), crushed
1¼ cups of milk (regular or vanilla soy)
2 tablespoons unsalted butter, melted

1. Preheat oven to 350 degrees. Spray loaf pan with no-stick cooking spray. Set aside.
2. Drain and rinse salmon. Beat 2 eggs with a dash of salt and pepper. Add to drained salmon and mix. Add dill, green onions, crackers, milk, and butter. Combine. If the loaf mixture becomes thick, add more milk. Should not be runny but have the consistency of cake batter.
3. Pour mixture into prepared loaf pan. Bake for 60 minutes or until wooden skewer inserted into middle of salmon loaf comes out clean. Place on rack and cool for 15 minutes.
4. Run a knife around the side of the loaf pan and turn out onto serving plate or board. Slice or leave whole. Garnish with fresh dill weed and my Simple Dill Sauce (see under The Basics). Serve with pita chips or sliced on a bed of lettuce greens.

Serves ten to twelve.

Cool Smoked Salmon Pizza

1 12-ounce, room-temperature pizza dough (see Pizza Dough
    under The Basics), prebaked and cooled
8 ounces cream cheese (fat-free, low-fat, or regular), softened
8 ounces smoked salmon or Whiskey-Soaked Salmon (see recipe
    in this chapter)
½ cup chopped roma tomatoes, cored with seeds removed
½ cup red onion, chopped
3 tablespoons capers
2 tablespoons fresh dill weed, chopped
Freshly grated Pecorino Romano cheese

1. Preheat oven to 450 degrees. Stretch room-temperature pizza dough
   into a thin round crust and place on a cornmeal-dusted pizza pan,
   parchment paper, or baking sheet. Do not use a rolling pin as this
   will push gases out of dough. Bake for 8–10 minutes until golden.
   Completely cool before assembling pizza.
2. Spread softened cream cheese over the cooled pizza crust. Top with
   smoked salmon and sprinkle with chopped tomatoes. Finish topping with onion, capers, and dill weed. Add freshly grated Pecorino
   Romano cheese before serving.

Serves six when cut into circular wedges.
May also be sliced into squares.

🍴 Supreme Chocolate Cake

4 cups cake flour
2 teaspoons baking soda
¾ teaspoon kosher salt
1 cup cocoa—
   Dutch processed
1 cup warm water
1 cup buttermilk
1 cup cool water
1 teaspoon pure vanilla extract

1 cup unsalted butter,
   room temperature
2 cups white sugar
1½ cups light brown sugar,
   packed down
4 large eggs, room temperature
½ cup bittersweet chocolate,
   chopped

Chocolate Buttercream Filling
Chocolate Ganache Topping

1. Preheat oven to 350 degrees.
2. Grease 14-inch round cake pan with butter and flour. Tap out any excess. Set aside.
3. Sift flour, baking soda, and salt into a bowl; set aside.
4. Whisk cocoa and warm water in a bowl; set aside.
5. In another bowl, whisk together buttermilk, cool water, and vanilla; set aside.
6. In bowl of electric mixer, with paddle attachment, add softened butter, white sugar, and light brown sugar. Beat about 2 minutes.
7. Turning mixer speed to low, add one egg at a time. Add additional eggs only after each is well combined. Beat 1 minute on medium after all eggs have been added.
8. Add cocoa mixture and beat on low until combined.
9. Add flour mixture and buttermilk mixture alternately—about 1 cup of each. Repeating until both mixtures are added.
10. Mix batter until smooth. Remove from mixer and gently fold in chopped chocolate.
11. Pour batter in pan and bake about 90 minutes or until toothpick/wooden skewer comes out clean. Do not overbake.
12. While cake is cooling prepare the filling and topping.

Chocolate Buttercream Filling

    1 cup unsalted butter, softened
    ¼ cup heavy cream
    ½ teaspoon pure vanilla extract
    ⅓ cup cocoa—Dutch processed
    4 cups confectioner's sugar

1. In bowl of electric mixer, with paddle attachment, add softened butter and mix until creamy.
2. Add cream and vanilla until mixed.
3. Stop mixer and add cocoa. Mix on low until blended and begin adding confectioner's sugar. Turn speed to high until well mixed.

Chocolate Ganache Topping

    4 cups heavy cream
    2 cups unsalted butter
    36 ounces bittersweet chocolate

1. Warm cream in heavy saucepan on low heat. Add butter and chocolate. Continually stir mixture over low heat until smooth. When almost all chocolate is melted, remove from heat and cool.
2. In bowl of electric mixer, with whisk attachment, whip until smooth.
3. With serrated knife, cut cake in half.
4. Spread Chocolate Buttercream filling on lower half of cake. Put the other half on top and press down gently with hands.
5. Pour Chocolate Ganache on top of cake and spread with spatula. Place in refrigerator and chill. After 10 minutes, add another layer of Chocolate Ganache and let set in refrigerator.
6. Remove and garnish with fresh red raspberries or other berries that are in season.

ϯ Tortilla Swirls

    1 cup sour cream (fat-free, low-fat, or regular)
    1 cup cream cheese (fat-free, low-fat, or regular), softened
    1 cup shredded cheddar cheese (fat-free, low-fat, or regular)
    ½ cup red onion, finely chopped
    1 6-ounce can black olives, drained and chopped
    2 large garlic cloves, minced
    8 fajita-style flour tortillas
    Picante sauce or salsa

1. Combine sour cream, cheeses, onion, olives, and garlic. Spread mixture on flour tortillas and roll. Wrap each rolled tortilla in plastic wrap and chill at least 6 hours or overnight.
2. Before serving, remove from refrigerator and slice into ½-inch slices. Arrange swirls into a pattern on serving platter and serve with picante sauce, salsa, guacamole, or Vidalia Onion Relish (see under Festival of the Moonflower).

⸘ Warm Spinach Dip

    1 medium yellow onion, chopped
    1½ cups button mushrooms, sliced
    ¼ cup unsalted butter
    2 tablespoons unbleached flour
    1 teaspoon kosher or Hawaiian salt
    1 teaspoon freshly ground black pepper
    ¼ teaspoon fresh basil, chopped
    ¼ teaspoon fresh oregano, chopped
    ¼ teaspoon fresh thyme, chopped
    ½ cup sour cream (fat-free, low-fat, or regular)
    1 pound fresh spinach, chopped
    1 cup of hand-packed mozzarella cheese, shredded

In a medium heavy-bottom sauce pan, melt butter. Add onions and mushrooms and cook over medium-high heat until onions are translucent. Add flour, salt, pepper, herbs, and sour cream. Turn heat down to low and stir in spinach. Pour spinach mixture in a small baking dish and top with cheese. Place under broiler until cheese melts. Serve warm with crusty bread, baked pita chips, or assorted crackers.

Gathering at Mokihana on the Island of Kauai

W HEN SOMEONE RETURNS from the Hawaiian Islands they tell you two things, the first being that they have truly found paradise and the second being how expensive food is there, whether in restaurants or grocery stores. Everyone I know who has been to Hawaii shares their astonishment at seeing the price of a carton of milk. My partner and I, along with the Benson women (Linda their mother, and sisters Lorna, Leslie, and Lanee'), decided that we wanted to go to Kauai for a week. I looked into lodging and found that hotel rooms were extremely expensive. After days of searching the Internet, I found a magnificent ocean-front house for rent on the south side of the island near Poipu Beach. The photographs of the house were amazing, which begged the question, "Does this place really exist?" After a couple of e-mail communications and checking with the Kauai Better Business Bureau, I was reassured that this paradise home, located in paradise, truly was standing and not just a grass shack enhanced by a computer.

After arriving on Kauai, I would have accepted a grass shack. It is one of the most beautiful places I've ever visited. I haven't traveled to all the lands of this planet yet, but I can say with confidence that the island of Kauai would be difficult to surpass. Immediately, I was struck by the lush foliage. The only main highway has crews in several locations chopping away the jungle as it attempts to reclaim the land that has become paved road. I noticed a colorful hedge of hibiscus as neatly trimmed as I would trim a boxwood hedge back at my home. The kindness of the people was the most abundant beauty on this island. The islanders want to share their happiness and graciousness with everyone they come in contact with. It is too beautiful not to be happy here, too rapturous not to be generous. Beauty does not always mean a mountain range or flowing streams. I remember the people of Kauai with fondness, and they are one of the main reasons I want to return there.

Graciousness and generosity, of course, do not always translate well to those visiting the island. I witnessed several tourists with extremely bad behavior. One situation involved a couple who had just arrived on the island and were on the way into a resort. They must have asked the shuttle driver to stop at a wonderful exotic vegetable and fruit stand, which I write about later in this chapter. I had been at the stand for a while, asking about the produce and chatting with the sociable owners. The young couple approached the stand and immediately began making unpleasant comments about the exotic names and the appearance of some of the produce. I saw the disappointment on the owners' faces. I also saw disgust and hurt in the owners' eyes. The young couple even turned to me and made comments, to which I replied that I thought it was beautiful produce. Fortunately, that response caused them to leave me alone. I wasn't going to be party to their negative observations. They left with an underripe pineapple, and the mood immediately improved. The point of this story is that I ask all who travel to be polite guests. Think of others' cities, states, islands, or countries as their home and remember that you are a guest with all the responsibilities of being a well-behaved visitor. It will make a difference. The power of graciousness and the phrase "thank you" is remarkable, and you will be thrilled at the reactions and generosity that are returned to you.

We had a fantastic vacation, and we all remarked, several times, that this was truly a *vacation* vacation. No work, lying by the ocean, sunshine daily, and paradise on all four corners of the island. Before we left for Hawaii I worked on an extensive menu and grocery list. After all the horror stories about the cost of food, I worried that we would overspend our vacation budget. I researched which supermarkets were located on Kauai and registered for a savings club card. I also viewed their weekly specials on the Internet. I downloaded a map, too, but later discovered that finding anything on Kauai was relatively easy because there are no large cities on the island.

Once we purchased our groceries, we returned to our house, unpacked, and I began the process of making dough for Grandma's Sticky Buns, Pizza Dough, and Hamburger Buns. We grilled potatoes, hamburgers, and sweet corn that first evening. While I sliced the potatoes, the girls started yelling because humpback whales were spouting and cresting out of the ocean as the sun began setting in the western sky. It was remarkable and a memory that I will never forget. I certainly didn't mind cooking with the Pacific Ocean in front of my food preparation area and on the other side, Flat-Top Mountain as my view over the kitchen sink. I couldn't have designed a more fabulous kitchen with a view.

The next morning we remarked on the convenience of being able to get out of bed in our robes and, as the girls put it, without having to "put our faces on" to have breakfast. We sat on the lanai (patio) and ate ham steaks, eggs, oatmeal, and Grandma's Sticky Buns. We also made coffee and drank juice. The morning was beautiful, and we ate and watched for whales. The convenience of having purchased groceries afforded us the luxury of gathering items for quick picnics or having snacks whenever we felt hungry. We made salads and stored them for lunch or marinated meats in simple sauces for supper on the lanai later. Many people I have told about purchasing groceries have replied that when they go on vacation they do not want to cook. I guess I have never considered cooking a chore or something I need a vacation from.

The other point I would like to make is the good deal of money we saved. We estimated that our group of six saved $1,450 for our entire week on Kauai. We even ate leftover Salmon Pizza and Shrimp Pizza before going to the airport. Another great aspect of buying groceries and cooking was that everyone took part in the making and in the gathering we had created in this house on the Pacific Ocean. It definitely was a group event, and it went on every day for seven days. When we did visit a restaurant, we didn't feel guilty about overspending a little.

Grocery List

The following is the list I prepared before we traveled to Kauai. I researched the ingredients of the recipes we chose and used an Internet grocery store to find the price of each item. This Internet grocery store has higher-end prices, which was better for averaging our foods costs. I prefer to budget too much rather than too little. You can always use the extra money for souvenirs or tropical cocktails after a day of snorkeling.

Part of my research included finding out what grocery stores were in the area. If you decide to purchase groceries while on vacation, check out the variety of stores where you're staying. I actually enjoy shopping in grocery stores in other cities or countries. In addition to my Internet research, I checked out a couple of travel books from my local library for suggestions about where to shop. Once you find stores you're interested in, check out their Web sites if they have them. I found two supermarkets in Waipouli, near Kapa'a, on Kauai. I visited their Web sites and found that they offered club cards, which I applied for. I also brought my own coupons. With the cards and coupons, we saved a total of $47.51, or 15 percent, off our total grocery bill of $324.24. And because we had budgeted for this expense, we charged to our credit card with a special rebate program and received the benefits. When I say that we budgeted for it, I mean that as soon as the bill arrived in the mail, we had the money set aside to pay it. No interest was charged, which kept our savings at 15 percent. Yes, we overspent from our original $170.23 budget, but we hadn't added in alcoholic beverages. We also found a special on several cases of diet soda, and some items we just decided we wanted to have on hand. We still averaged $7.72 per person per day for food. Not bad. When we ate on the island of Oahu, we averaged $16.50 per person per meal, a difference of $49.50 compared to $7.72 for each day. This certainly made our vacation much more enjoyable, but also healthier. A good many of the staples we obtained were low-fat or fat-free products. The produce, meats, and seafood were the freshest we could locate and prepared with little or no fat, making each meal nourishing and good for us. I actually lost several pounds with the added activity (swimming, hiking—and shopping!) of being there. The one feature we didn't go without was great taste. Remember, if it doesn't taste good, it doesn't go into my recipe collection or on my table.

Grocery List and "High-End" Budget for Each Item on the List

MEATS AND SEAFOOD

- Shrimp—$10.98/2 pounds
- Chicken breast—$5.99/pound
- Turkey, chicken, roast beef deli meats—$5.99/pound
- Crab meat—$2.99/pound
- Ham steaks—$1.59/6 ounces
- Bacon—$4.49/pound
- Ground beef—$2.69/pound, 10 percent fat
    - Total = $34.72

FRUITS AND VEGETABLES

- Parsley—.99
- Garlic—.79
- Lemon—.99
- White and red potatoes—1.99/bag each
- Onions—$2.00/bag
- Red onions—.59
- Celery—$1.29
- Japanese cucumbers—.59 each
- Cabbage—$1.70
- Pineapple—$3.99
- Carrots—.79/bag
- Pecans—$4.49
- Kiwis—$1.99/bag
- Raisins—$2.99 canister
- Asparagus or stir-fry vegetables—$3.99/bunch
- Green onions—.99
- Sprouts—$1.49
- Regular mushrooms and canned—$1.69
    - Total = $33.34

DAIRY

- Eggs—.99
- Fat-free margarine—$1.89
- Parmesan cheese—$3.00 wedge
- Reduced-fat shredded cheese (mild cheddar and mozzarella)—
  2 for $7.00
- Provolone cheese—$3.25 ½ pound
- Soy milk—$3.19 large carton
- Fat-free sour cream—$2.00
    - Total = $21.32

STAPLES

- Flour—$4.00/10 pounds
- Cane sugar—$1.89/4 pounds
- Olive oil—$6.99
- Vegetable oil—$1.89
- Kosher salt—$1.99
- Yeast—$5.00
- Cooking spray—$3.59
- Bread crumbs—$1.99
- Balsamic vinegar—$3.99
- Regular vinegar—$1.69
- Cider vinegar—$1.99
- Rice vinegar—$3.19
- Fat-free mayo—$3.97 large jar
- Fat-free salad dressing—$1.97 small jar
- Pickle relish—$1.99
- Honey—$3.29
- Brown cane sugar—$1.39
- Picante sauce—$4.00
- Baked cheese snacks, tortilla chips, and potato chips—
  $3.99 a bag/$11.97
- Oatmeal—$2.50
- Tortillas—$1.39

- Soy sauce—$1.99
- Cornstarch—$1.69
- Soda (diet and regular)—$1.50 2 liter bottle/$3.00

    Total = $77.35

PAPER OR PLASTIC

- Plastic wrap—$3.50

    - Total = $3.50

- Grand total budget for groceries = $170.23 or $28.37 per person or $4.05 per day per person. Note: This does not include coupons or savings from Safeway Club card. This is a "high-end" budget.

- Actual grand total for groceries = $324.24 with extras such as beer, wine, snacks, and other items we saw and just had to have. However, we saved $47.51, or 15 percent, of our grocery bill by using their club card and manufacturer's coupons.

- $54.04 per person or $7.72 per day per person.

Here is a list of the herbs and spices that I brought along in my suitcase in small jars and plastic bags. This may seem extreme, but we saved our group around $30 by bringing our own.

- Black pepper
- Rosemary
- Sage
- Basil
- Thyme
- Garlic powder
- Oregano
- Ground ginger
- Paprika
- White pepper
- Cinnamon

SUGGESTED SELECTIONS FOR YOUR
GATHERING AWAY FROM HOME

This is the menu that I created for our trip. It provided meals, snacks, and picnics for six Minnesotans for one week on the island of Kauai. It was terrific to have leftover meals to munch on, and we also celebrated our last evening on the island by having "leftover" night to finish items we had stored during the week.

- BREAKFAST

  - Grandma's Sticky Buns
  - Oatmeal
  - Juice and Fruit
  - Bread, Eggs, and Bacon

- LUNCH

  - Crab Rolls
  - Red River Red Potato Salad
  - Cole Slaw
  - Hawaiian Cole Slaw
  - Tuna Salad

- EVENING

  - Grilled Portobello Mushroom Burgers
  - Hawaiian Cucumber Salad (Sunomono)
  - Chicken Taco Pizza
  - Chicken or Seafood Fajitas
  - Potato Fritters (see under Gathering for a Backyard Barbecue)
  - Chicken Asparagus

- ◆ Beef Asparagus
- ◆ Stir-Fried Rice
- ◆ Aloha Ranch Chicken Spears

◆ SNACKS

- ◆ Soda (diet and regular)
- ◆ Microwave Popcorn (94 percent fat-free)
- ◆ Baked Chips

Grandma's Sticky Buns

Hmmm . . . the recipe title just doesn't sound right, but it is how I have identified these delicious chewy rolls ever since I was a child. All rolls and buns were named after family members. We had Grandma's Sticky Buns, Berget Fish's Buns, and so on. You get the picture, but don't try visualizing too hard. Call them what you want, but you can enjoy these "full fat" or almost fat-free. I have prepared them both ways, and nothing is lost in the translation. Wrapped tightly, these satisfying rolls will keep for up to three days.

¼ cup unsalted butter or margarine (regular, low-fat or fat-free)
1 cup milk (regular or vanilla soymilk)
½ cup water
¼ honey
1½ teaspoons kosher or Hawaiian salt
2 large eggs
2 tablespoons or 2 packets yeast
5 to 5½ cups unbleached flour

1. Melt butter or margarine in a medium sauce pan over low heat. Add milk and water. Remove from heat and add honey, salt, and eggs. Making sure the liquids are just lukewarm, stir in yeast.
2. Transfer liquids to a bowl and add flour. Combine until bread whisk or spoon is no longer effective. Kneading, continue adding flour until you have a stiff dough, about 10 minutes. Cover and let rise until double in volume.

Caramelized Mixture

½ cup unsalted butter or margarine (regular, low-fat, or fat-free)
1 cup dark brown sugar
2 tablespoons water

Heat all ingredients in a small saucepan and stir to blend. Set aside.

FINAL PREPARATION

¼ cup unsalted butter or margarine (regular, low-fat, or fat-free)
Dark brown sugar
Cinnamon
1 cup golden raisins (optional)
1 cup chopped pecans

1. Cut dough into two equal portions. Roll out each portion into approximately a 6-inch-by-24-inch rectangle. Spread ¼ cup butter or margarine on each rolled-out piece of dough. Sprinkle each portion with brown sugar, cinnamon, and raisins.
2. Roll up each portion of dough like a jelly roll.
3. Pour caramelized mixture into two standard loaf pans, 13- × 9-inch baking pan, or 14-inch round cake pan. Sprinkle chopped pecans evenly in pan.
4. Cut rolled dough into 16 pieces. Place in prepared bread/cake pan.
5. Cover and let rise until doubled in volume—about 1 hour. Preheat oven to 350 degree; bake 25–30 minutes. Turn out on to serving platter or decorative cake plate.

Oatmeal

I enjoy old-fashioned oatmeal very much. It starts the day off right, and I don't feel hungry until it is time for lunch. The experts were correct when they told us that breakfast was the most important meal of the day. The U.S. Food and Drug Administration claims that some foods such as oatmeal have been proved to actually reduce blood cholesterol levels, especially LDL (the "bad" cholesterol), while maintaining levels of HDL (the "good" cholesterol). "Soluble fiber from oatmeal in a diet low in saturated fat and cholesterol may reduce the risk of heart disease." So, I say, get in the habit of eating a bowl of oatmeal every day. I add vanilla soy milk, honey from the island of Kauai (imagine the taste as the bees visit all the exotic flowers on the island!), raisins, and a sprinkle of cinnamon. It's delicious, great for you, and a fantastic way to start each morning. It is also very easy to prepare while you are on vacation.

Juice and Fruit

While on the island of Kauai we were privileged to have many varieties of juice to choose from daily. A mixture of passion fruit, orange, and guava juices ("POG") was my favorite. While traveling, juice is a good source of vitamins but can also be a light snack instead of a bag of chips. If you are fortunate to be on an island, visit an exotic vegetable and fruit stand and experience the diverse selection of produce. I found a stand that was housed under a grass roof. The owners were two elderly women, and I asked plenty of questions on each visit. I would bring them plastic grocery bags to recycle every time I dropped by. I took my time and asked the pronunciation of every piece of fruit. I sampled several, and my favorite was rambutans. Encased in fibrous red shells, rambutans offer a sweet fruit the size of a hard-boiled egg once they are sliced open. There is a hard seed inside that you must eat around or cut out. I often reminisce with affection about these astonishing, modest fruits because they symbolize a unique element of my trip to Kauai. It was my approach to "soaking up local color," as Lucy Ricardo *(I Love Lucy)* once put it. We also purchased a good deal of freshly picked sweet corn, which we roasted on the grill. I believe our troop's favorite fruit was fresh pineapple. It was the sweetest pineapple we had ever tasted. We honestly needed to consume it over a sink it was so succulent. Make your trip extra special and adventurous by shopping at the local farmers' markets or stands. Ask questions on how to pronounce the names, the origins, and how to prepare their crop. The locals will be more than happy to acquaint you with their harvest.

Rambutan, *Nephelium lappaceum,* drawn by Dr. M. J. Dijkman

Bread, Eggs, and Bacon

This recipe was something Grandma would cook up, and she said it best, "In a jiffy." I always have day-old peasant, Italian, or regular bread on hand in my kitchen, and this is a great way to finish off bread before I give it to the birds. This is also another recipe that is easy to prepare while on vacation if you have a kitchen available. It is practical and inexpensive because the ingredients will last several days in a refrigerator. It's also very tasty.

    1 loaf of crusty or day-old bread, cut into 1-inch slices with the
        center hollowed out
    1 large egg per person
    3 slices of pork bacon or turkey bacon per person

"One of the worst mistakes you can make as a gardener is to think you're in charge."

—JANET GILLESPIE

1. Spray a heavy-bottom skillet or griddle with cooking spray. Place bread slice in pan and cook over medium-low heat. After 1 minute, crack an egg into the hollowed-out center. Cook until the egg is almost cooked through.
2. Place slices of bacon alongside bread and cook until crisp.
3. With a spatula, turn bread and egg over to cook on opposite side.
4. Drain bacon on paper towels and keep warm until bread and egg are done.
5. Serve immediately, placing bacon over bread and egg.

Crab Rolls

1 recipe for Crab Salad (see under The Academy Awards Gathering)
6 Frankfurter, hoagie, bratwurst rolls or buns

Prepare Crab Salad as directed. After chilling, spread on sliced rolls or buns. Serve with pickle spears and baked potato chips.

Serves six.

Red River Red Potato Salad

I use a one-gallon ice cream bucket to mix the dressing and later add the vegetables. This is an easy way to prepare this recipe. Place a secure cover over the bucket and refrigerate. This also offers an easy way to transport your salads for a picnic or outing. I use ice cream buckets for food storage but also as compost buckets to store kitchen scraps that I later transfer to the garden compost area. It is just one more way to recycle items we would normally throw away.

2½ pounds red potatoes, cooked and cut into bite-size pieces
2 large hard-boiled eggs, chopped
1 cup mayonnaise (regular, low-fat, or fat-free)
2 tablespoons vinegar
2 teaspoons kosher or Hawaiian salt, additional for salting water
1 teaspoon sugar
1 large garlic clove, minced
½ teaspoon freshly ground pepper
2 celery stalks, finely chopped
1 medium onion, finely chopped
¼ cup flat-leaf Italian parsley, finely chopped

1. Bring potatoes to a boil over high heat. Salt water and reduce heat to medium high. Slow-boil potatoes until fork tender—about 45 minutes. Add eggs to potato water and continue to slow-boil for an additional 10 minutes. Remove from heat and let rest for 10 minutes. Drain and rinse with cool water.
2. While the potatoes are boiling prepare dressing. In a large mixing bowl, add mayonnaise, vinegar, salt, sugar, garlic, and pepper. Blend well and set aside to let flavors mature.
3. Meanwhile, slice celery, onion, and parsley. Prepare cooled potatoes and eggs. Combine all ingredients with dressing and toss until well coated. Chill for at least 2 hours before serving.

Serves eight to ten.

"The first day of spring is one thing, and the first spring day is another. The difference between them is sometimes as great as a month."

—HENRY VAN DYKE

⨍ Cole Slaw

As with the Red River Red Potato Salad, I use a one-gallon ice cream bucket to first mix the dressing and then to add the vegetables. This step makes for effortless mixing and storing. As with all recipes in this book, use the freshest, best-quality ingredients for the absolute finest taste. I choose savoy cabbage from Europe for its buttery and nutty flavors. At times, it is difficult to find but do try because you will not believe a cabbage would offer so much flavor. Depending on my frame of mind, I at times will use half green cabbage and half red cabbage. This makes a vibrant salad.

> 2 cups mayonnaise (regular, low-fat, or fat-free)
> 2 tablespoons cider vinegar
> 2 tablespoons sugar
> 1 large garlic clove, minced
> 1 teaspoon kosher or Hawaiian salt
> 1 teaspoon ground white pepper, Indonesia coarse grind if available
> 3 large carrots, shredded or cut into matchsticks
> 1 large sweet onion, thinly sliced and separated
> 1 savoy cabbage, shredded

1. In a large mixing bowl, add mayonnaise, vinegar, sugar, garlic, salt, and pepper. Blend well and set aside to let flavors mature.
2. Shred carrot and slice onion. With a large sharp knife, slice cabbage in half. Thinly slice each half and cross slice to create large shreds. Repeat with second half of cabbage. Also leave some longer strands of cabbage to toss in your slaw.
3. Combine all ingredients with dressing and toss until well coated. Chill for at least 2 hours before serving.

Serves eight to ten.

Hawaiian Cole Slaw

I highly recommend that you prepare this recipe with fresh pineapple. The natural sweetness is complemented by the mayonnaise and vinegar sourness. All these flavors blend so perfectly together. This slaw is wonderfully refreshing on picnics or on the lanai watching the humpback whales cresting in the blue Pacific Ocean. Aloha!

1 cup mayonnaise (regular, low-fat, or fat-free)
2 tablespoons milk (regular, low-fat, or vanilla soy)
1 tablespoon white vinegar
1 teaspoon sugar
½ teaspoon kosher or Hawaiian salt
¼ teaspoon freshly ground black pepper
1 head savoy, green, or red cabbage
2 cups fresh or canned pineapple, drained if using canned
Dash of smoked Spanish or regular paprika

1. In a large mixing bowl, combine mayonnaise and milk. Add vinegar, sugar, salt, and pepper. Blend well and set aside to let flavors mature.
2. With a large sharp knife, slice cabbage in half. Thinly slice each half and cross slice to create large shreds. Repeat with second half of cabbage. Also leave some longer strands of cabbage to toss in your slaw. Slice rough rind from pineapple, core, and cut into bite-size chucks.
3. Combine all ingredients with dressing and toss until well coated. Chill for at least 2 hours before serving. Sprinkle with paprika before serving.

Serves eight to ten.

"Gardeners are generous people and perennials, which grow and multiply, help foster these instincts."

—DAVID SCHEID

🖋 Tuna Salad

I have been making this tuna salad since I was around the age of thirteen. Grandma shared this recipe one day with me when she first became ill. We had been working in the garden, and she was beginning to feel some pain. We were both a bit hungry, and I told her that I would make some cheese sandwiches. She replied that she felt like having tuna for lunch and asked if I would prepare this salad. Grandma preferred a famous-name salad dressing, but I've used both dressing and mayonnaise, depending on what I had available. Grandma taught me several sandwich fillings. I have probably prepared this recipe more than any other because it is so simple yet so gratifying.

> 1 6–7 ounce package or can of premium chuck light tuna in water, drained
> 3 tablespoons Grandma's Sweet Cucumber Relish (see under Festival of the Moonflower)
> 2 tablespoons salad dressing or mayonnaise (regular, low-fat, or fat-free)
> Pinch of kosher or Hawaiian salt (optional)
> Lettuce
> Tomato, sliced
> Red onion, thinly sliced
> 4 onion or kaiser rolls

1. In a small mixing bowl, flake tuna with a fork. Add relish, salad dressing, and salt. Stir well.
2. Slice rolls and layer with lettuce, tomato, and onion. Spoon tuna salad on top and serve.

Serves four.

Variation: Create a Tuna Salad Melt by substituting whole wheat bread for rolls. Spread margarine or butter on each slice of bread. Omit lettuce and spoon tuna salad on bread. Top with cheddar cheese slices (regular, low-fat, fat-free, or soy). Cover with bread slice and place on preheated grill or skillet sprayed with cooking spray. Turn once and cook until cheese begins to melt.

Grilled Portobello Mushroom Burgers

Chad and I have adopted one day each week that is meatless. I grill portobello mushrooms in place of hamburgers or steak burgers and serve with a salad and Potato Fritters (see under Gathering for a Backyard Barbecue). The marriage of good-quality balsamic vinegar and olive oil is startling. If you cannot find fresh basil or oregano, dried will do. Simply increase your marinating times by 10 minutes to rehydrate the herbs. I truly hope you enjoy these "meatless" delights.

4 large portobello mushroom caps
⅓ cup balsamic vinegar
3 tablespoons extra virgin olive oil
2 teaspoons fresh basil, finely chopped
2 teaspoons fresh oregano, finely chopped
2 large garlic cloves, minced
½ teaspoon kosher or Hawaiian salt
½ teaspoon freshly ground black pepper
4 slices havarti, provolone, or Swiss cheese
4 large hamburger buns (see under The Basics) or onion rolls

1. Using a one-gallon food storage bag or container with a lid, combine vinegar, oil, basil, oregano, garlic, salt, and pepper. Blend well. Lay mushroom caps, smooth side up, in container. Secure bag or container and carefully turn until mushrooms are covered in marinade. Let rest at room temperature for 10 minutes. Turn again and let rest again for 10 minutes.
2. Spray barbecue grill or stove top skillet grill with cooking spray. Preheat heat source to a medium heat.
3. Using tongs, place marinated mushroom caps on grill. Use remaining marinade for basting. Grill each side for 5–8 minutes and turn to prevent burning. May turn numerous times until each side is tender. Brush with marinade on each turn. Place cheese slice on mushroom caps during the last couple minutes of grilling.

⸙ Hawaiian Cucumber Salad (Sunomono)

While on the island of Kauai, I found Japanese cucumbers at my favorite vegetable stand near Poipu Beach. They are called *suhyo* and are a longtime favorite in Japan. The suhyo plant produces long, slender cucumbers, about 1¼ inches round by 18 inches long. The suhyo's skin is dark green and has small spines. The flesh is firm, crisp, and delicious. It is used raw in salads, dips, and sandwiches, as well as in Asian cooking. Selecting good-quality Japanese cucumbers is similar to choosing English cucumbers. The Japanese variety is firm, thin, long, and an even dark-green color. Avoid cucumbers that are soft, yellow, or wrinkled on the ends.

1 teaspoon fresh ginger, grated
4 tablespoons rice vinegar
2 tablespoons sugar
1 teaspoon kosher or Hawaiian salt
2 medium suhyo, Japanese, cucumbers, thinly sliced
1 cup small shrimp, cooked and tails off

1. In a mixing bowl, combine ginger, vinegar, sugar, and salt. Stir until salt and sugar are dissolved.
2. Gently blend cucumbers and shrimp with vinegar mixture. Chill at least 1 hour before serving.

Serves six to eight.

⸙ Chicken Taco Pizza

This is a recipe that I prepare every two weeks on Friday or Saturday evening, on the weekends that we have our daughter, Heather. I created this pizza a year or so ago because both Chad and Heather love "Make your own taco night." This recipe is a variation on that theme except that we use pizza dough. I still set the table with fat-free sour cream, torn lettuce, black olives, marinated mushrooms, and extra shredded fat-free cheeses. Most of the time, I am the only person at the table partaking of the "extras." Heather spoons half the container of sour cream on top of her piece of pizza and Chad the other half of the container. However you top this pizza it's delicious using low-fat or fat-free products. It's our way of eating healthily but not giving up flavor.

> 1 12-ounce, room-temperature pizza dough (see Pizza Dough
> under The Basics)
> 2 tablespoons good-quality extra virgin olive oil
> 2 boneless, skinless chicken breasts cut into bite-size pieces
> 1 large red onion, diced
> 1 cup medium/mild picante or salsa sauce
> Kosher or Hawaiian salt and freshly ground black pepper
> 1 cup shredded mozzarella cheese (regular, low-fat, or fat-free)
> ½ cup shredded cheddar cheese (regular, low-fat, or fat-free)
> ¼ cup freshly grated Pecorino Romano cheese

1. Preheat oven to 450 degrees. Stretch room-temperature pizza dough into a thin round crust and place on a cornmeal-dusted pizza pan, parchment paper, or baking sheet. Do not use a rolling pin as this will push gases out of dough.
2. Drizzle stretched pizza dough with extra virgin olive oil. Using pastry brush spread oil around dough including edge. Set side.
3. Using a heavy-bottom skillet over medium-high heat, drizzle with olive oil. Add cut-up chicken and sauté until golden. Combine onions and stir occasionally until pink. Sprinkle with salt and pepper. Remove from heat.
4. Evenly spread picante or salsa over prepared pizza dough. Distribute the chicken and onion mixture over sauce. Cover with shredded and grated cheeses.
5. Slide pizza into the hot oven and bake for 20–30 minutes. Baking times will depend on thickness of crust and amount of toppings.
6. Transfer to a cutting board and brush edge of crust with olive oil to add shine and flavor.

Serves six.

⸮ Chicken or Seafood Fajitas

I will admit it, these are not true fajitas as they are historically known, but because it seems that anything wrapped in a tortilla shell is now called a fajita, this is my version. The original fajitas were made with beef called skirt steak that was tough and had a lot of membranes. Because of this the beef was marinated for several hours. In most cases, marinating was for an overnight period or longer.

I have added red onions to this recipe because they give it tang. I cut the onion in half and toss it in the pan so that there are large slices of onion. I have also added red and green bell peppers. Try adding zucchini, cooked carrots, cabbage, and other vegetables that you enjoy.

> 2 boneless, skinless chicken breasts
> > *or*
> ½ pound medium shrimp, clean and deveined with tails off
> 1 tablespoon extra virgin olive oil
> 1 large red onion
> 1 10–12-ounce jar medium/mild picante or salsa sauce
> ½ cup shredded Mexican or cheddar cheese (regular, low-fat, or fat-free)
> 4 large flour or corn tortillas

1. In a heavy-bottom skillet over medium heat, add oil and swirl around to coat skillet. Once oil is heated, add chicken or shrimp. Cook until chicken is golden or shrimp just turns pink.
2. Reduce heat to medium low and add onion. Cook, stirring occasionally, until onion begins to turn purplish pink but is still crunchy. Remove from heat.
3. Add picante or salsa and blend well. Set aside.
4. Heat tortillas in a microwave or over a low flame on a gas stove. Fill with meat mixture and sprinkle with shredded cheese. Roll or wrap and serve.

Serves four.

⸘ Chicken Asparagus

When asparagus is past its prime, I use zucchini. Then when bell peppers or green beans are in season, I simply adjust the ratio of chicken to vegetables.

  1 tablespoon good-quality soy sauce
  1 tablespoon cornstarch
  ¼ teaspoon sugar
  ½ cup chicken broth (see under The Basics) or water
  4 tablespoons vegetable or peanut oil, divided
  1 large garlic clove, minced
  1 teaspoon ginger, whole root grated or powdered
  3 to 4 medium boneless, skinless chicken breasts, cut into bite-size
     pieces
  ⅛ teaspoon white pepper, Indonesian coarse grind (if available)
  1 pound asparagus
  1 large onion, cut into quarters and petals separated
  2 tablespoons water
  Dash of sugar

1. In a small bowl or measuring cup mix a cooking sauce by combining soy sauce, cornstarch, sugar, and broth. Set aside. Stir well before adding to meat and vegetables.

2. Heat a wok or deep frying pan over medium-high heat. Add 2 tablespoons oil. When oil begins to heat, add garlic and ginger. Stir immediately and do not let garlic burn or brown as it will become bitter. Add chicken and stir-fry until cooked though, about 5–8 minutes. Remove chicken from pan.

3. Add 2 tablespoons oil to pan and heat. Add asparagus and onion and stir-fry for about 2 minutes. Add water, sprinkle with sugar, cover, and cook for 3 minutes. This will steam the vegetables until crisp but tender. Return chicken to pan. Add cooking sauce. Stir-fry all ingredients until sauce begins to bubble and thicken.

Serves four.

⸕ Beef Asparagus

As with the Chicken Asparagus recipe, when asparagus is past its prime or out of season, substitute other vegetables or ones that you like best with beef. I also enjoy trying a variety of onions such as Vidalia or other sweet onions, along with red onions to add zip to the dish. I've enjoyed adding snow peas and bok choy cabbage also. Both Chicken and Beef Asparagus are versatile recipes that are easy to adapt for any hard-to-please family.

> 1 tablespoon soy sauce
> 1 tablespoon cornstarch
> ¼ teaspoon sugar
> ⅔ cups beef broth or water, divided
> 4 tablespoons vegetable or peanut oil, divided
> 1 large garlic clove, minced
> 1 pound top round steak, cut into bite-size cubes
> 1 pound asparagus, cut into ½-inch slanting slices
> 1 large onion, cut into quarters and petals separated

1. In a small bowl or measuring cup mix a cooking sauce by combining soy sauce, cornstarch, sugar, and ½ cup beef broth or water. Set aside. Stir well before adding to meat and vegetables.
2. Heat a wok or deep frying pan over medium-high heat. Add 2 tablespoons oil. When oil begins to heat add garlic. Stir immediately and do not let garlic burn or brown as it will become bitter. Add beef and stir-fry until cooked though, about 8 minutes. Remove beef from pan.
3. Add 2 tablespoons oil and heat. Add asparagus and onion and stir-fry for about 2 minutes. Add remaining beef broth or water, cover, and cook for 3 minutes. This will steam the vegetables until crisp but tender. Return beef to pan. Add cooking sauce. Stir-fry all ingredients until sauce begins to bubble and thicken.

Serves four.

⨍ Stir-Fried Rice

This is a great recipe for using up leftover turkey, chicken, beef, ham, or pork. I usually prepare it with all the vegetables, but any additions to this recipe are welcome.

>   8 ounces bean sprouts, rinsed and drained
>   4 tablespoons vegetable or peanut oil, divided
>   2 large eggs, slightly beaten
>   1 4-ounce can or jar of mushrooms, drained
>   3 cups cooked white or brown rice
>   3 tablespoons soy sauce
>   ¼ teaspoon white pepper, Indonesia coarse grind if available
>   1 cup cooked turkey, chicken, beef, ham, or pork (optional)
>   3 green onions, chopped with greens

1. Rinse bean sprouts in cold water and drain. Heat wok or large skillet over medium heat. Add 1 tablespoon oil and rotate pan to coat all sides. Add eggs and stir until thickened but still moist. Remove eggs and set aside.
2. Add 1 tablespoon oil to pan and rotate to coat all sides. Add bean sprouts and mushrooms. Stir-fry for about 5 minutes or until heated throughout. Remove from pan to a colander or strainer.
3. Add 2 tablespoons oil to pan. Rotate to coat all sides. Add rice and stir-fry for 2 minutes. Add soy sauce and white pepper. Continue to stir-fry for another 2 minutes or until soy sauce is well incorporated.
4. Add optional cooked meat at this time. Return bean sprouts, mushrooms, and eggs to pan. Add green onions. Stir-fry for another 2 minutes.

*Serves eight. For storage, cover tightly and refrigerate
no longer than 24 hours.*

⸎ Aloha Ranch Chicken Spears

1 fresh pineapple
4 boneless, skinless chicken breasts
½ cup teriyaki sauce
1 tablespoon of unsalted butter
Pinch of sugar
½ cup of flour
2 eggs, slightly beaten
½ cup dried bread crumbs
1 (1-ounce) packet of Hidden Valley Ranch Salad Dressing and
    Seasoning Mix
1 1-ounce packet of Hidden Valley Original Ranch Dips Mix
1 8-ounce container sour cream (fat-free, low-fat, or regular)
Wooden skewers
2 tablespoons vegetable oil

1. Slice pineapple in half, lengthwise. Place one half of the pineapple in plastic wrap and refrigerate until dish is ready for assembly. Using a paring knife, carefully cut out pineapple pulp from other half of the pineapple. Mash half of the pineapple pulp to extract juice. Wrap other section in plastic wrap and refrigerate until chicken is ready to cook. Mix pineapple juice and teriyaki sauce in baking dish. Cut chicken breasts into thirds, horizontally, and place in pineapple juice/teriyaki marinade. Cover baking dish and refrigerate overnight or at least 4 hours. (I save the half-hallowed out pineapple skin as a serving bowl for dressing to dip chicken spears.)

2. Heat tablespoon of unsalted butter in a large nonstick skillet over medium heat. Remove plastic wrap from second section of pineapple pulp. Slice, peel, and core into 12 bite-size cubes and place in heated skillet. Sprinkle with a pinch of sugar and cook until caramelized, 4 to 5 minutes on each side. Transfer to a warming dish, cover, and set aside.
Note: Caramelized pineapple chucks are optional. You may omit this step and simply garnish the end of each skewer with fresh pineapple chucks.

3. Remove chicken from marinade and thread each piece on a wooden skewer. Combine bread crumbs and packet of Hidden Valley seasoning mix in shallow bowl or pie plate. Cover both sides of chicken in flour. Dip chicken in the beaten egg, and then dredge in bread crumb mixture, turning to coat both sides.

4. Heat 2 tablespoons oil in a large nonstick skillet over medium heat. Place 3 chicken spears in skillet; cook until golden, 1 to 2 minutes on each side. Using tongs, transfer browned spears to paper towel to drain excess oil. Repeat until all spears are browned.

5. Remove plastic wrap from refrigerated pineapple half and place fruit side down on serving platter. Push blunt ends of browned chicken spears through pineapple skin so that it resembles a pin cushion. Garnish end of each skewer with a caramelized pineapple cube.* Serve plain or with Hidden Valley Original Ranch Dips Mix (made with sour cream).

Makes twelve chicken spears.

American Pie Festival Gathering

A GATHERING DOES NOT NECESSITATE that everyone coming together be familiar with one another. One of my ideal gathering arrangements is to assemble several people who don't know each other. The occasion will yield many future friends by the time it has ended. I was fortunate to be a guest at such a gathering while at the 2005 Great American Pie Festival sponsored by Crisco and held in Celebration, Florida. I entered six of my dessert pies in the American Pie Council/ Crisco National Pie Championship Amateur Division. I returned home with two ribbons on my first try: a third place white ribbon for my Hana Hou! Daiquiri Pie and a second place red ribbon and Crisco gift basket for my Razzle Dazzle Berry Pie. There is nothing that can surpass leaving a gathering with a gift in hand from your host. Thank you, American Pie Council and Crisco, for making Chad and me feel so welcome.

As a teenager growing up in the Red River Valley of North Dakota, I enjoyed baking pies and conceiving new recipes that would blend garden favorites in interesting ways. Now that I live in Saint Paul, Minnesota, I still rely on what is growing in my garden but also on what is being offered at the Saint Paul Farmers' Market.

A favorite gathering concept of mine is to host a pie festival of my own. I ask everyone to bring a pie. Whether a savory pie, vegetable pie, pizza pie, or dessert pie, each guest is encouraged to bring his or her favorite. Those guests who do not bake are asked to contribute wine or salad. There are no requirements; however, I try to coordinate what people bring so that we have a good variety to offer everyone at the gathering—you do not want six apple pies. The invitation states that a store-bought pie is just as fine as a homemade one. You can make your own crust or use a ready-made crust bought from your local market. The gathering itself is a celebration of friendships, of bonds we have formed through caring and respect. It does not need to be hindered by getting distressed over what to bring.

As I stated, not all the pies at your festival gathering need to be dessert pies. I have produced a variety of savory pies filled with meats, seafood, or vegetables. Perhaps you may want to create a theme. You may choose to have a couple of friends over for dinner rather than a party. If your theme is the South Seas, choose my Crab Pie and serve a citrus pie such as Hana Hou! Daiquiri Pie or Key Lime Delight Pie for dessert. My hearty Manitoba Meat Pie deserves a robust fruit-filled tart pie such as Razzle Dazzle Berry Pie or Grandma Anderson's Rhubarb-Strawberry Pie.

Encourage your friends or family to come over early and aid you in the pie-baking process. The more the merrier, I always say. An extra benefit from assembling pies together is the exchange of dialogue that will take place in your kitchen. There may also be someone in your inner circle who has baking secrets they will share during this rendezvous. The more pies you make, the more proficient you'll become. Yes, there is an art to making a good pie, but, like finger-painting, your creations will become prettier the more you practice. The mystery will fade away and pie baking will become a breeze. You may also look forward to baking a pie as much I do.

As I have mentioned in the other chapters and in my introduction, using ready-made products from your local market is not a felony. A couple of years ago I did just that. I used a ready-made crust when I prepared my Vidalia Onion Pie for a dinner to celebrate my and Chad's anniversary. Leave it to Chad to announce at the table that had I made my own crust it would have been a better-tasting pie. Chins hit the table and this revelation, of course, opened up the discussion for the next ten minutes about my not baking my own crust. I find it interesting, at times, that I have developed a reputation for never using ready-made products. Oh, if they only knew. Not that it is shocking to make use of ready-made food items; it's just that the bar has been raised so very high that people expect me to make everything from scratch. Go ahead and make my recipes with ready-made food items and add your own touches. The main idea is to awaken the next morning and declare with a smile, "Didn't we have fun yesterday?"

So make a pie for yourself and your guests. Bake a pie for the person who just moved into your neighborhood, or bake a treat for someone who is feeling low because of a tragedy in their family or for some other reason. There is nothing as satisfying as the finished pie cooling in your kitchen and when you present it to the intended person. I guarantee that you will lean over that pie several times during the cooling process and inhale the fragrance of your labor. And while you are at it, enter your pie in a local contest, county fair, or your state fair. I cannot express how much fun it is to compete at a fair. Yes, I have taken it to the national level, but that's just how I like to do things. Enter your pie. If you are a determined pie baker, join the American Pie Council.

The American Pie Council is the only organization committed to preserving our country's pie heritage and promoting Americans' love affair with pies. Designed to raise awareness, enjoyment, and consumption of pies, the council offers both personal and commercial memberships. Benefits range from the exchange of recipes to in-store coupons and ideas from other pie lovers. The commercial member can participate in a variety of network and promotional opportunities sponsored by the council. Important to the commercial member is the combined effort of the members of the American Pie Council to grow and improve the pie industry.

The American Pie Council hosts the National Pie Championships, which have been bringing together commercial, professional, and amateur bakers from across the United States and Canada since 1995. The council has created a standard of quality in pie making and has a well-established record in the pie-judging field. The competition is part of the Great American Pie Festival, which has been hosted in Celebration, Florida, for four consecutive years. The family-oriented festival features entertainment, baking demonstrations, crafts and games, pie-eating contests, children's pie making, and the "Never Ending Pie Buffet," which allows visitors to sample pies created by professional and commercial bakers. For more information on the National Pie Championships, the Great American Pie Festival, or all things pie related, please visit www .piecouncil.org. Their motto is "In Pie We Trust." Bake a pie today.

SUGGESTED LIST OF PIES FOR YOUR GATHERING:

- Belmont Road Chicken Pie
- Crab Pie
- Easter Pie
- Manitoba Meat Pie
- Sombrero Cheese Pie
- Saint Paul Farmers' Market Vegetable Pie
- Vidalia Onion Pie
- Apple Butter Hand Pies
- Chocolate-Covered Cherry Pie
- Grandma Anderson's Rhubarb-Strawberry Pie
- Hana Hou! Daiquiri Pie ("One More Time" in Hawaiian)
- Key Lime Delight Pie
- Peachy Keen Pecan Pie
- Razzle Dazzle Berry Pie
- Red River Valley Vanilla Cream Pie

Time-Saving Tip: Make pie crusts ahead of time, wrap in plastic wrap, and freeze.

⸕ Belmont Road Chicken Pie

Crust

3 cups all-purpose flour
1 tablespoon sugar
1 teaspoon kosher or Hawaiian salt
½ cup all-vegetable shortening, cut into small pieces
½ cup cold unsalted butter, cut into small pieces
½ cup cold water
1 large egg yolk and 1 teaspoon water for egg wash

1. All ingredients should be cold. Combine all the dry ingredients in a large mixing bowl. Add shortening and butter. Using a pastry blender, cut in the shortening and butter until the mixture resembles coarse meal.
2. Drop by drop, add the cold water. Mix in with the fingertips, not with the hands as the palms will warm the dough. Continue mixing in water until the dough begins to hold together without being sticky but not crumbly.
3. Divide dough into two pieces and place each in plastic wrap. Fold over plastic wrap and press down to form a disk. This will make rolling out easier after chilling. Finish wrapping in plastic and place in the refrigerator for at least 1 hour.
4. Lightly spray a 9-inch pie plate with butter or vegetable cooking spray. Roll out dough and place in pie plate. Return to the refrigerator until filling is ready. Roll out top crust.

Filling

1 (3½ pound) chicken, cut-up fryer
1 large onion, diced and divided
1 carrot, thinly sliced
1 celery stalk, chopped
1½ teaspoons kosher or Hawaiian salt

½ teaspoon fresh French or English thyme leaves
3 cups water
½ cup fresh button mushrooms, sliced
¼ cup unsalted butter
3 tablespoons all-purpose flour
¼ teaspoon white pepper, Indonesian coarse grind
Dash freshly ground black pepper
Dash freshly ground nutmeg
½ cup fresh or frozen peas, thawed if frozen

1. Preheat oven to 425 degrees. In a stock pot or Dutch oven over medium-high heat, bring to a boil chicken, ¾ cup onions, carrot, celery, salt, thyme, and water. Boil for 5 minutes. Cover pot and reduce heat to simmer until chicken and carrots are tender; about 45 minutes. Remove from heat and strain through a colander lined with cheesecloth. When cool enough to handle, remove chicken meat from the bone. Shred or cut up into bite-size pieces. Set aside.

2. In same stock pot or Dutch oven, melt butter over medium heat. Add remaining onions and mushrooms. Sauté until onions are translucent and mushrooms release their moisture. Add flour, nutmeg, white and black pepper. Stir until well blended. Measure 1½ cups strained chicken broth. Add to onion/mushroom/flour mixture and blend well. Continue stirring over medium heat until thickened. Fold in chicken and peas.

3. Pour mixture and spread evenly in prepared pie crust. Brush egg wash on bottom edge and carefully attach top crust. This will "glue" the bottom and top crust together and prevent the filling from bubbling out through the sides. Create a decorative edge and brush with remaining egg wash. Cut slits in top to release steam. Bake for 30 minutes or until crust is golden. Remove from oven and cool on a rack for 20 minutes before serving.

Serves eight to ten.

⨍ Crab Pie

Crust

    1½ cups all-purpose flour
    ½ tablespoon sugar
    ½ teaspoon kosher or Hawaiian salt
    ¼ cup cold all-vegetable shortening, cut into small pieces
    ¼ cup cold unsalted butter, cut into small pieces
    ¼ cup cold water
    1 large egg yolk and 1 teaspoon water for egg wash

1. All ingredients should be cold. Combine all the dry ingredients in a large mixing bowl. Add shortening and butter. Using a pastry blender, cut in the shortening and butter until the mixture resembles coarse meal.
2. Drop by drop, add the cold water. Mix in with the fingertips, not with the hands as the palms will warm the dough. Continue mixing in water until the dough begins to hold together without being sticky but not crumbly.
3. Place dough in plastic wrap. Fold over plastic wrap and press down to form a disk. This will make rolling out easier after chilling. Finish wrapping in plastic and place in the refrigerator for at least 1 hour.
4. Lightly spray a 10-inch pie plate with butter or vegetable cooking spray. Roll out dough and place in pie plate. Create a decorative edge and return to the refrigerator until filling is ready.

Filling

    2 tablespoons extra virgin olive oil
    ½ cup carrot, finely chopped
    ¼ cup green onions, chopped with greens
    1 teaspoon fresh dill weed
    1 teaspoon fresh basil
    1 pound crab meat

1 12-ounce can evaporated milk
5 large eggs
3 tablespoons dry sherry
1 tablespoon prepared mustard
½ teaspoon kosher or Hawaiian salt
¼ teaspoon freshly ground black pepper

1. Preheat oven to 325 degrees. Heat olive oil in a heavy-bottom skillet over medium heat. Sauté carrots until tender, about 10 minutes. Add onions, dill, and basil and continue cooking for 2 minutes.
2. Remove vegetable and herb mixture from heat. Fold in crab meat and pour into prepared pie crust.
3. In a medium mixing bowl, whisk milk, eggs, sherry, mustard, salt, and pepper. Pour evenly over crab mixture in pie crust. Brush edge of pie crust with egg wash. Bake for 50 minutes or until a skewer inserted in the center comes out clean. Remove from oven and let cool on a rack for 15 minutes before slicing.

Serves eight.

Easter Pie

This savory pie might sound as if it is only for the spring holiday, but I make it any day I believe my guests want a substantial dining experience. It is by no means low-fat but is perhaps my most scrumptious of pies. Easter Pie is delicious either warm, room temperature, or reheated. Store in the refrigerator.

Crust

3 cups all-purpose flour
1 tablespoon sugar
1 teaspoon kosher or Hawaiian salt

½ cup cold all-vegetable shortening, cut into small pieces
½ cup cold unsalted butter, cut into small pieces
½ cup cold water
1 large egg yolk and 1 teaspoon water for egg wash

1. All ingredients should be cold. Combine all the dry ingredients in a large mixing bowl. Add shortening and butter. Using a pastry blender, cut in the shortening and butter until the mixture resembles coarse meal.
2. Drop by drop, add the cold water. Mix in with the fingertips, not with the hands as the palms will warm the dough. Continue mixing in water until the dough begins to hold together without being sticky but not crumbly.
3. Divide dough into two pieces and place each in plastic wrap. Fold over plastic wrap and press down to form a disk. This will make rolling out easier after chilling. Finish wrapping in plastic and place in the refrigerator for at least 1 hour.
4. Lightly spray a 10-inch pie plate with butter or vegetable cooking spray. Roll out dough and place in pie plate. Return to the refrigerator until filling is ready. Roll out top crust just before placing in oven. Makes pastry for 10-inch double-crust pie.

Filling

1 tablespoon extra virgin olive oil
2 pounds Italian sausage, chopped
¼ pound prosciutto, chopped
½ pound ham, diced
2 pounds whole-milk ricotta cheese, preferably ewe's milk ricotta
12 ounces mozzarella cheese, shredded
¼ teaspoon kosher, Hawaiian, or sea salt, depending on your taste
¼ teaspoon freshly ground black pepper
5 large eggs
1 tablespoon flat-leaf Italian parsley, chopped
¼ cup freshly grated Parmigiano-Reggiano cheese

1. Preheat oven to 400 degrees. Heat olive oil in a heavy-bottom skillet over medium heat. Add sausage and cook until almost browned. Add prosciutto and ham. Sauté until heated through, approximately 5 minutes. Remove from heat and let cool. Drain grease if necessary.

2. In a mixing bowl combine ricotta, mozzarella, salt, and pepper. Add eggs, one at a time, mixing each until combined. Add cooled meat mixture to cheese mixture, stirring until blended. Fold in parsley and Parmiginao-Reggiano cheese.

3. Pour filling into dough-lined pie plate. Brush egg wash around edge of crust. This will "glue" the bottom and top crust together and prevent the filling from bubbling out through the sides. Cut slits in the top crust to release steam or cut a hole in the very center.

4. I like to use any remaining dough to decorate the edge of the pie. Lightly knead remaining dough together and roll out a rectangle at least 10 inches long. Using a pastry cutter or knife, cut three strips of dough. Braid together and twist. Lay braided dough on top of the outer edge of the pie. Brush crust and braid with egg wash.

5. Place pie in oven and bake for 15 minutes. Reduce oven temperature to 325 degrees. Bake for 45 minutes or until crust is golden. Remove from oven and let cool on a rack for 15 minutes. Slice and serve with my Tuscan Tomato Sauce (see under The Basics).

Serves eight.

⸕ Manitoba Meat Pie

When I lived in Grand Forks, North Dakota, I loved driving north to Winnipeg, Manitoba. Sometimes I would visit twice a month. A very good friend who lived in Winnipeg made this pie on the weekends that I would visit. He would invite all his friends over for what he titled "Hangover Pie." My traveling buddy Mark Johnson loved this pie and got the recipe from our Canadian friend. Mark and I worked on variations, but I liked this one the best. It's very hearty and will make you feel warm all over. Enjoy! And Mark, we miss you very much.

Crust

    3 cups all-purpose flour
    1 tablespoon sugar
    1 teaspoon kosher or Hawaiian salt
    ½ cup cold all-vegetable shortening, cut into small pieces
    ½ cup cold unsalted butter, cut into small pieces
    ½ cup cold water
    1 egg yolk and 1 teaspoon water for egg wash

1. All ingredients should be cold. Combine all the dry ingredients in a large mixing bowl. Add shortening and butter. Using a pastry blender, cut in the shortening and butter until the mixture resembles coarse meal.
2. Drop by drop, add the cold water. Mix in with the fingertips, not with the hands as the palms will warm the dough. Continue mixing in water until the dough begins to hold together without being sticky but not crumbly.
3. Divide dough into two pieces and place each in plastic wrap. Fold over plastic wrap and press down to form a disk. This will make rolling out easier after chilling. Finish wrapping in plastic and place in the refrigerator for at least 1 hour.
4. Lightly spray a 9-inch pie plate with butter or vegetable cooking spray. Roll out dough and place in pie plate. Return to the refrigerator until filling is ready. Roll out top crust.

Filling

1 pound red potatoes, diced
1½ teaspoons kosher or Hawaiian salt
2 cups water
1 pound lean ground beef or meatless ground beef
1 large onion, diced
2 celery stalks, chopped
3 large garlic cloves, minced
Dash of cinnamon
¼ teaspoon ground cloves
2 teaspoons fresh French or English thyme leaves
1 teaspoon fresh sage, shredded
1 teaspoon freshly ground black pepper
1 cup of red wine

1. Place potatoes in a large saucepan and cover with water. Bring to a boil over medium-high heat. When water begins to boil, add salt. Boil hard for 5 minutes and reduce heat to low and slow boil for about 45 minutes or until fork tender but not breaking apart. Remove from heat and drain but save ¼ cup of the potato water. Set aside.
2. In a heavy-bottom skillet over medium heat, brown beef. Add onions, celery, garlic, cinnamon, cloves, thyme, sage, and pepper. Stir to combine and slowly add ¼ cup potato water and wine. Let mixture come to a rolling boil and reduce heat and simmer until liquid has evaporated; about 30 minutes. Remove from heat.
3. Divide boiled potatoes and mash one half and leave the other half in chunks. When liquid has evaporated from the meat mixture, stir in mashed potatoes. Carefully fold in potato chunks. Let cool to room temperature.

"Gardening is medicine that does not need a prescription . . .
And with no limit on dosage."

—AUTHOR UNKNOWN

---

4. Preheat oven to 450 degrees. Brush bottom pie crust with egg wash, including edges. Brushing egg wash around edges of crust will "glue" the bottom and top crust together and prevent the filling from bubbling out through the sides. Spoon mixture into prepared crust and spread evenly. Carefully attach top crust and crimp edges together. Create a decorative edge and slit top crust to release steam. Bake for 15 minutes. Reduce oven temperature to 350 degrees and continue baking for 30 minutes or until crust is golden. Remove from oven and cool on a rack 20 minutes before serving. Tastes great with Tuscan Tomato Sauce (see under The Basics).

Serves eight to ten.

Sombrero Cheese Pie

Crust

    1½ cups all-purpose flour
    ½ tablespoon sugar
    ¼ teaspoon kosher or Hawaiian salt
    ¼ cup cold all-vegetable shortening, cut into small pieces
    ¼ cup cold unsalted butter, cut into small pieces
    ¼ cup cold water
    1 large egg yolk and 1 teaspoon water for egg wash

1. All ingredients should be cold. Combine all the dry ingredients in a large mixing bowl. Add shortening and butter. Using a pastry blender, cut in the shortening and butter until the mixture resembles coarse meal.
2. Drop by drop, add the cold water. Mix in with the fingertips, not with the hands as the palms will warm the dough. Continue mixing in water until the dough begins to hold together without being sticky but not crumbly.
3. Place dough in plastic wrap. Fold over plastic wrap and press down to form a disk. This will make rolling out easier after chilling. Finish wrapping in plastic and place in the refrigerator for at least 1 hour.

4. Lightly spray a 9-inch pie plate with butter or vegetable cooking spray. Roll out dough and place in pie plate. Return to the refrigerator until filling is ready. Makes pastry for 9-inch single-crust pie.

Filling

> 2 7-ounce packages of shredded cheddar cheese (salsa with tomato and jalapeño pepper–flavored; approximately 4 cups)
> ⅓ cup finely chopped flat-leaf parsley
> ¼ cup minced onion
> ½ teaspoon kosher or Hawaiian salt
> ½ teaspoon ground mustard
> ½ teaspoon Worcestershire sauce
> 3 eggs
> ¼ cup evaporated milk
> ½ cup sour cream
> Grape or cherry tomatoes
> Jalapeño peppers
> Freshly ground black pepper

1. Mix shredded cheese, parsley, onion, salt, mustard, Worcestershire sauce, eggs, milk, and sour cream. Pour in unbaked pie crust. Bake at 350 degrees for 25 minutes.
2. Cut tomatoes into thin slices. Overlap slices around the outer edge of the pie to form a tomato wreath. Sprinkle with salt and pepper and return to oven. Bake for 15 minutes.
3. Cool pie and garnish with sliced and seeded jalapeño peppers. Serve with salsa and a salad.

Serves 8

Variation—Italian Cheese Pie: Replace cheese in recipe with 2 7-ounce packages of mozzarella and Asiago with roasted garlic flavored shredded cheese or similar. Keep the tomatoes, but instead of jalapeño peppers as your garnish, top with fresh basil leaves. Serve with marinara sauce and a salad.

Saint Paul Farmers' Market Vegetable Pie

My grandmother made this fantastic vegetable pie after she visited Allard's Vegetable Market in East Grand Forks, Minnesota. It was located on the "Point" and set up in Allard's garage. As a young boy, I remember the fragrance of fresh dirt clinging to the newly picked produce. It still enlivens me, and when I pick from my own garden, I reminisce about going to Allard's with Mom or Grandma. I love this recipe and will change it to suit the vegetables available at the farmers' market near my home in Highland Park—the Saint Paul Farmers' Market. It's a phenomenal place with live music on Saturday morning, freshly squeezed lemonade to refresh you while you browse, and some of the best honeys, jams, vegetables, live plants, and Asian delicacies. The market is an amazing plethora of the best the earth will yield to those who care for it.

Crust

 1½ cups all-purpose flour
 ½ tablespoon sugar
 ½ teaspoon kosher or Hawaiian salt
 ¼ cup cold all-vegetable, cut into small pieces
 ¼ cup cold unsalted butter, cut into small pieces
 ¼ cup cold water
 1 large egg yolk and 1 teaspoon water for egg wash

1. All ingredients should be cold. Combine all the dry ingredients in a large mixing bowl. Add shortening and butter. Using a pastry blender, cut in the shortening and butter until the mixture resembles coarse meal.
2. Drop by drop, add the cold water. Mix in with the fingertips, not with the hands as the palms will warm the dough. Continue mixing in water until the dough begins to hold together without being sticky but not crumbly.
3. Place dough in plastic wrap. Fold over plastic wrap and press down to form a disk. This will make rolling out easier after chilling. Finish wrapping in plastic and place in the refrigerator for at least 1 hour.

4. Lightly spray a 9-inch pie plate with butter or vegetable cooking spray. Roll out dough and place in pie plate. Return to the refrigerator until filling is ready. Makes pastry for 9-inch single-crust pie.

Filling

4 tablespoons unsalted butter, divided
1 small head of savoy cabbage, shredded; regular is fine if
    savoy is unavailable
1 large onion, chopped
1 large garlic clove, minced
2 teaspoons fresh basil, chopped
1 teaspoon kosher or Hawaiian salt
½ teaspoon freshly ground black pepper
Dash of white pepper, Indonesian coarse grind, if available
8 ounces fresh mushrooms, any variety, sliced
8 ounces cream cheese (regular, low-fat, or fat-free),
    room temperature
4 large eggs, hard-boiled and sliced
Several sprigs of fresh dill weed

1. Preheat oven to 350 degrees. In a heavy-bottom stock pot or Dutch oven, melt 2 tablespoons butter over medium heat. Add cabbage and onions, Stir occasionally until cabbage wilts and onions are translucent. Stir in garlic, basil, salt, black pepper, and white pepper. Pour into a bowl and set aside.
2. Melt remaining 2 tablespoons butter and add mushrooms. Stir and cook until mushrooms release their moisture. Fold mushrooms into cabbage and onion mixture.
3. Brush prepared bottom pie crust with egg wash, including edges. Spread cream cheese over the bottom pie crust. Layer the eggs slices over the cream cheese and sprinkle with dill weed. Spoon vegetable mixture into crust and spread evenly. Brush egg wash around edges of crust. This will "glue" the bottom and top crust together and prevent the filling from bubbling out through the sides. Carefully attach top crust and crimp edges. Create a decorative edge and cut slits in the

top to release steam. Brush top with remaining egg wash. If you have small cookie cutters that resemble vegetables; get creative and cut out remaining dough and paste on top of crust with egg wash.

4. Bake for 50 minutes or until crust is golden. Remove from oven and cool on a rack for 20 minutes before serving.

Serves eight to ten.

Vidalia Onion Pie

Crust

1½ cups all-purpose flour
½ tablespoon sugar
½ teaspoon kosher or Hawaiian salt
¼ cup cold all-vegetable shortening, cut into small pieces
¼ cup cold unsalted butter, cut into small pieces
¼ cup cold water
1 egg yolk and 1 teaspoon water for egg wash

1. All ingredients should be cold. Combine all the dry ingredients in a large mixing bowl. Add shortening and butter. Using a pastry blender, cut in the shortening and butter until the mixture resembles coarse meal.

2. Drop by drop, add the cold water. Mix in with the fingertips, not with the hands as the palms will warm the dough. Continue mixing water in until the dough begins to hold together without being sticky but not crumbly.

3. Place dough in plastic wrap. Fold over plastic wrap and press down to form a disk. This will make rolling out easier after chilling. Finish wrapping in plastic and place in the refrigerator for at least 1 hour.

"Wouldn't it be better to simply live what you believe, and teach by example . . . rather than by preaching."

—DARYL RYMAN

4. Lightly spray a deep 9-inch pie pan or 8 ½-inch fluted flan pan. Roll out dough and place in pie plate. Return to the refrigerator until filling is ready. Makes pastry for 9-inch single-crust pie.

Filling

2 pounds Vidalia onions, thinly sliced
½ cup unsalted butter
3 large eggs, beaten
1 cup sour cream
3 tablespoons all-purpose flour
¼ teaspoon of kosher or Hawaiian salt
½ teaspoon freshly ground black pepper
Freshly grated Parmesan

1. Preheat oven to 450 degrees. Brush egg wash on the inside of pie crust. Return to refrigerator until filling is ready.
2. Over medium heat, melt butter. Add onions and sauté until translucent. Do not brown. Combine eggs, sour cream, and flour. Add to onion mixture. Season with salt and pepper and pour into chilled pie crust. Top with grated cheeses.
3. Bake for 20 minutes. Reduce oven temperature to 325 degrees for the last 20 minutes or until center is set.

Serves eight.

⸙ Apple Butter Hand Pies

3 cups all-purpose flour
1 tablespoon sugar
1 teaspoon kosher or Hawaiian salt
½ cup cold all-vegetable shortening, cut into small pieces
½ cup cold unsalted butter, cut into small pieces
½ cup cold water

2 large egg yolks and 2 teaspoons water for egg wash
3 cups Apple Butter (see under The Basics)
Vanilla sugar, for sprinkling
Cinnamon, for sprinkling

1. All ingredients should be cold. Combine all the dry ingredients in a large mixing bowl. Add shortening and butter. Using a pastry blender, cut in the shortening and butter until the mixture resembles coarse meal.

2. Drop by drop, add the cold water. Mix in with the fingertips, not with the hands as the palms will warm the dough. Continue mixing in water until the dough begins to hold together without being sticky but not crumbly.

3. Divide dough into two pieces and place each in plastic wrap. Fold over plastic wrap and press down to form a disk. This will make rolling out easier after chilling. Finish wrapping in plastic and place in the refrigerator for at least 1 hour.

4. Preheat oven to 350 degrees. Lightly flour your work surface and roll out one half of the refrigerated dough to a thickness of ⅛ to ¼ inch. With a 4½- to 5-inch baking ring or biscuit cutter, cut circles from rolled-out dough. Carefully move circles to a parchment- or Silpat-lined baking pan. Chill in refrigerator for 30 minutes. Roll out remaining dough, cut circles, and chill.

5. Remove chilled dough from refrigerator and spoon 2 tablespoons of apple butter in center of dough circle. Spread evenly but leave ½-inch space from edge. Brush edge with egg wash and fold in half so that the bottom and top edge come together evenly. Press with finger tips to seal. Crimp to create a decorative edge. Continue until you finish off all remaining dough. Return hand pies to refrigerator and chill for 20 minutes.

6. Remove chilled pies and brush with egg wash. Sprinkle with vanilla sugar and cinnamon. Bake for about 30 minutes or until crust turns golden. Remove from oven and cool on a rack 15 minutes before serving.

Serves about twelve.

⸕ Chocolate-Covered Cherry Pie

Crust

¼ cup chopped pecans

Approximately 35 chocolate wafers or 2 cups chocolate
cookie crumbs

2 tablespoons dark brown sugar

1 tablespoon all-purpose flour

¼ teaspoon ground cinnamon

Pinch of Hawaiian or kosher salt, pressed to a fine powder
with mortar and pestle

⅓ cup unsalted butter, melted

1. Preheat oven to 350 degrees. Spray 9- or 10-inch pie plate with cooking spray and set aside.
2. Add chocolate wafers to food processor or crush with mortar and pestle. Pulse until wafers are broken down. Add pecans and continue pulsing until finely chopped. Add brown sugar, flour, cinnamon, and salt. Mix well. Pour butter over crumb mixture and process until mixture begins to hold together.
3. Spread crumb mixture in pie plate, pressing into the bottom and up the side.
4. Bake for 10–12 minutes. Cool and place in refrigerator for 10 minutes before filling.

Cherry Filling

½ cup sugar

½ cup water

12 ounces pitted cherries, fresh or frozen

¼ teaspoon ground cinnamon

3 teaspoons cornstarch

1. In a small saucepan over medium heat, stir sugar and water until dissolved. Bring to a boil and cook until liquid is reduced by half. Add cherries and cinnamon and cook for 2 minutes.

2. Add cornstarch and combine until thickened. Cool completely before adding to filling.

Chocolate Filling

> 1 11½-ounce package double chocolate chips
> 1 cup heavy whipping cream, whipped
> ½ cup milk
> 1 envelope unflavored gelatin
> 2 8-ounce packages cream cheese, softened
> 1 cup sour cream
> ½ teaspoon almond extract

1. Melt chocolate chips in double boiler, stirring until smooth. Set aside.
2. Whip cream and set aside.
3. In a saucepan combine milk and gelatin. Cook over low heat, stirring constantly until gelatin dissolves. Set aside.
4. Beat cream cheese, sour cream, and melted morsels in a mixing bowl until fluffy. Beat in gelatin mixture and almond extract. Fold the whipped cream into chocolate mixture.

ASSEMBLY

Sweetened Whipped Topping

> ½ cup heavy whipping cream
> ½ teaspoon pure vanilla extract
> 2 tablespoons confectioner's sugar
> Semisweet chocolate curls

Pour half of the chocolate mixture into the pie crust. Pour cherry filling on top of chocolate layer and pour remaining chocolate mixture on top. Run spatula along edge of crust and chocolate filling to seal cherry filling under. Chill at least 4 hours or overnight. Garnish with whipped topping and chocolate curls.

Serves eight to ten.

Grandma Anderson's Rhubarb-Strawberry Pie

I believe Grandpa planted a patch of mouth-watering rhubarb next to the clothesline on purpose so that Grandma would bake him this pie whenever she hung clothes and glanced at the jam-packed rhubarb ready for baking. This one is an absolute must if you love dessert pie.

Crust

> 3 cups all-purpose flour
> 1 tablespoon sugar
> 1 teaspoon kosher or Hawaiian salt
> ½ cup cold all-vegetable shortening, cut into small pieces
> ½ cup cold unsalted butter, cut into small pieces
> ½ cup cold water
> 1 egg yolk and 1 teaspoon water for egg wash

1. All ingredients should be cold. Combine all the dry ingredients in a large mixing bowl. Add shortening and butter. Using a pastry blender, cut in the shortening and butter until the mixture resembles coarse meal.
2. Drop by drop, add the cold water. Mix in with the fingertips, not with the hands as the palms will warm the dough. Continue mixing in water in until the dough begins to hold together without being sticky but not crumbly.
3. Divide dough into two pieces and place each in plastic wrap. Fold over plastic wrap and press down to form a disk. This will make rolling out easier after chilling. Finish wrapping in plastic and place in the refrigerator for at least 1 hour.
4. Lightly spray a 9-inch pie plate with butter or vegetable cooking spray. Roll out dough and place in pie plate. Return to the refrigerator until filling is ready. Roll out top crust. Using a pastry cutter, cut strips for a lattice top. For something special, twist your lattice strips and then create your lattice weave. If using a full crust, cut slits in the top. Makes pastry for 9-inch double-crust pie.

Filling

2 cups fresh rhubarb, sliced into 1-inch pieces
2 cups fresh strawberries, sliced
1½ cups sugar
Pinch of kosher or Hawaiian salt
⅓ cup all-purpose flour
½ teaspoon almond extract
2 tablespoons unsalted butter
Vanilla sugar for sprinkling

1. Preheat oven to 400 degrees. In mixing bowl, gently blend rhubarb, strawberries, sugar, salt, flour, and almond extract.
2. Pour mixture into prepared pie crust. Dice butter and place around top of fruit mixture. Brush egg wash around edges of crust. This will "glue" the bottom and top crust together and prevent the filling from bubbling out through the sides. Cover with top crust and brush with remaining egg wash. Sprinkle with vanilla sugar.
3. Bake for 45 minutes or until crust is golden and fruit mixture is tender and bubbly. Remove from oven and cool on a rack. Serve with butter pecan or vanilla ice cream.

Serves eight.

⸖ Hana Hou! Daiquiri Pie—
Hawaiian for "One More Time"

2005 Winner, National Pie Championship, Third Place in the "Open" Category at the American Pie Festival

Crust

2 cups flaked coconut
4 tablespoons unsalted butter, melted

Combine the coconut and melted butter in a small bowl. Press into the bottom and up the side of an 8- to 9-inch pie plate. Bake at 325 degrees until the coconut is lightly browned, about 15 minutes. Turn half way through baking time for even browning of coconut. Cool completely while preparing filling.

Topping

½ cup large flaked coconut, lightly toasted

(Toast at the same time as the crust to garnish the pie.)

Lime Filling

⅔ cup sugar
1 envelope unflavored gelatin
¼ teaspoon Hawaiian salt
⅓ cup freshly squeezed lime juice, key lime preferably
⅓ cup water
3 large egg yolks, slightly beaten
½ teaspoon grated lime peel
¼ cup light rum
3 large egg whites
6 tablespoons superfine baker's sugar

1. Combine sugar, gelatin, and salt in a medium saucepan. In a small bowl, stir together lime juice, water, and egg yolks just enough to mix. Stir into sugar mixture. Cook on low heat, stirring constantly, until the mixture bubbles, thickens slightly, and coats a silver spoon.
2. Remove pan from heat; stir in lime peel and rum. Chill, stirring occasionally, until it has the consistency of corn syrup.
3. Beat egg whites until soft peaks form; gradually beat in sugar and beat until stiff peaks form but egg whites are still glossy. Fold into thickened gelatin mixture. Chill until the mixture mounds.

Lemon Filling

¾ cup sugar
3 tablespoons cornstarch
¼ teaspoon Hawaiian salt
¾ cup water
1 tablespoon unsalted butter
⅓ cup freshly squeezed lemon juice
1 teaspoon grated lemon peel
4 drops yellow food coloring

1. Combine sugar, cornstarch, and salt in a medium saucepan. Gradually stir in water. Cook over medium-low heat, stiffing constantly, until mixture boils and thickens. Boil 1 minute.
2. Remove from heat. Add butter, stirring until it melts. Add lemon juice, grated lemon peel, and food coloring and stir until smooth. Refrigerate until mixture has cooled.

ASSEMBLY

First, spoon lemon filling into cooled pie shell. Cover with lime filling and sprinkle with toasted coconut. Chill several hours or overnight before serving. Decorate to make look like a Daiquiri cocktail with twisted lemon and lime wedges and cherries skewed on paper umbrellas.

Serves eight.

⸘ Key Lime Delight Pie

Crust

2 cups all-purpose flour
½ cup chilled unsalted butter, diced
2 tablespoons sugar
2 large egg yolks
Pinch of kosher or Hawaiian salt
4–6 tablespoons cold water

1. Sift the flour into a mixing bowl. Using a pastry blender, "cut in the fat"—blend in the chilled butter until it resembles coarse meal. Add the sugar, egg yolks, salt, and water. Mix to a soft dough.
2. Roll out the pastry on a lightly floured surface and use to line a deep 9-inch pie pan or 8 ½-inch fluted flan pan, allowing the excess pastry to hang over the edge. Prick the pastry bottom and chill for 30 minutes.
3 Preheat the oven to 400 degrees. Trim the excess pastry from around the edge of the pastry shell. Line the pastry shell with parchment and baking beans or beads.
4. Bake the shell for 10 minutes. Remove the paper and beans/beads and return to the oven for 10 more minutes. Cool.

Filling

4 large eggs, separated
1 14-ounce can condensed milk
Grated zest and juice of 3 Key limes
2 tablespoons superfine baker's sugar

1. Lower the oven temperature to 325 degrees. Make the filling by beating the egg yolks in a large bowl until light and creamy. Beat in the condensed milk. Add the lime zest and juice. Mix well and continue to beat until the mixture is thick.
2. Beat egg whites until they form stiff peaks. Slowly add the sugar just until combined. Fold into the lime mixture.
3. Pour the lime filling into the baked crust. Bake for 20–25 minutes, or until filling is set and begins to brown. Remove and cool, about one hour. Chill in refrigerator for at least 2 hours.

Topping

1¼ cups heavy whipping cream
2 tablespoons confectioner's sugar
1 teaspoon pure vanilla extract
2–3 Key limes, thinly sliced
Lime zest and mint leaves for decoration

Before serving, whip the heavy cream, confectioner's sugar, and vanilla extract. Spoon or fill pastry bag to decorate edge of pie with whipped cream. Cut the lime slices from the center to the edge and twist. Arrange the lime slices between puffs of whipped cream. Lightly sprinkle Key lime zest and delicately place mint leaves in puffs of whipped cream to accent the pie.

Serves eight.

✶ Peachy Keen Pecan Pie

Crust

> 1½ cups all-purpose flour
> ½ tablespoon sugar
> ½ teaspoon kosher or Hawaiian salt
> ¼ cup cold all-vegetable shortening, cut into small pieces
> ¼ cup cold unsalted butter, cut into small pieces
> ¼ cup cold water
> 1 large egg yolk and 1 teaspoon water for egg wash

1. All ingredients should be cold. Combine all the dry ingredients in a large mixing bowl. Add shortening and butter. Using a pastry blender, cut in the shortening and butter until the mixture resembles coarse meal.
2. Drop by drop, add the cold water. Mix in with the fingertips, not with the hands as the palms will warm the dough. Continue mixing in water until the dough begins to hold together without being sticky but not crumbly.
3. Place dough in plastic wrap. Fold over plastic wrap and press down to form a disk. This will make rolling out easier after chilling. Finish wrapping in plastic and place in the refrigerator for at least 1 hour.
4. Lightly spray a 9-inch pie plate with butter or vegetable cooking spray. Roll out dough and place in pie plate. Return to the refrigerator until filling is ready. Makes pastry for 9-inch single-crust pie.

Filling

 3 large eggs
 ⅔ cup sugar
 ⅔ cup dark corn syrup
 ⅓ cup unsalted butter, melted
 1 teaspoon pure vanilla extract
 ½ teaspoon kosher or Hawaiian salt
 ⅔ cup fresh peaches, sliced in half
 1½ cups pecan halves, divided

1. Beat eggs, sugar, corn syrup, butter, vanilla, and salt with whisk until combined and foamy. Stir in peaches and 1 cup of pecans.
2. Brush pastry with egg wash and pour filling into pastry-lined pie plate. Place remaining ½ cup of pecan halves decoratively on top of filling and carefully transfer to oven.
3. Preheat oven to 375 degrees. Bake until filling is set, 35–40 minutes. Cool completely before cutting. Serve with whipped cream.

Serves eight.

𝑓 Razzle Dazzle Berry Pie

2005 Winner, National Pie Championship, Second Place in the "Fruit/Berry" Category at the American Pie Festival

Crust

 3 cups all-purpose flour
 1 tablespoon sugar
 1 teaspoon kosher or Hawaiian salt
 ½ cup cold all-vegetable shortening, cut into small pieces
 ½ cup cold unsalted butter, cut into small pieces
 ½ cup cold water
 1 large egg yolk and 1 teaspoon water for egg wash
 Vanilla sugar, for sprinkling

1. All ingredients should be cold. Combine all the dry ingredients in a large mixing bowl. Add shortening and butter. Using a pastry blender, cut in the shortening and butter until the mixture resembles coarse meal.

2. Drop by drop, add the cold water. Mix in with the fingertips, not with the hands as the palms will warm the dough. Continue mixing in water until the dough begins to hold together without being sticky but not crumbly.

3. Divide dough into two pieces and place each in plastic wrap. Fold over plastic wrap and press down to form a disk. This will make rolling out easier after chilling. Finish wrapping in plastic and place in the refrigerator for at least 1 hour.

4. Lightly spray a 9-inch pie plate with butter or vegetable cooking spray. Roll out dough and place in pie plate. Return to the refrigerator until filling is ready. Roll out top crust. Using a pastry cutter, cut strips for a lattice top. If using a full crust, cut slits in the top. Makes pastry for 9-inch double-crust pie.

Filling

1 cup sugar
Dash of kosher or Hawaiian salt
¼ cup cornstarch
½ teaspoon ground cinnamon
1 cup blueberries
1½ cups sliced strawberries
1 cup blackberries
1 cup red raspberries
½ cup water
2 tablespoons freshly squeezed lemon juice, about ½ a large lemon
2 tablespoons unsalted butter

1. In a heavy-bottom saucepan, combine sugar, salt, cornstarch, and cinnamon. Stir in berries. Add water and lemon juice. Cook over medium heat just to the boiling point. Stir filling gently so as not to

crush the raspberries. Push with the back of a spoon or carefully swirl saucepan to shift the mixture to prevent scorching.

2. Pour into chilled pie shell; dot with butter and top with crust. Apply egg wash and sprinkle with vanilla sugar. Bake at 350 degrees for about 45 minutes or until the crust is golden.

Serves eight.

f Red River Valley Vanilla Cream Pie

Crust

> 2 cups all-purpose flour
> ½ cup chilled unsalted butter, diced
> 2 tablespoons sugar
> 2 large egg yolks
> Pinch of kosher or Hawaiian salt
> 4–6 tablespoons cold water

1. Sift the flour into a mixing bowl. Using a pastry blender, "cut in the fat"—blend in the chilled butter until it resembles coarse meal. Add the sugar, egg yolks, salt, and water. When adding water, add the least amount and then add more as needed. Mix with fingertips to create soft dough. Do not use hands as palms will warm the dough. Let dough rest in refrigerator for 15 minutes.

2. Roll out the pastry on a lightly floured surface and use to line a 9-inch pie plate, allowing the excess pastry to hang over the edge. Trim the excess pastry from around the edge of the pastry shell. Create a handsome pastry edge and prick the pastry bottom. Chill for 30 minutes.

3. Preheat the oven to 400 degrees. Line the pastry shell with parchment and baking beans or beads.

4. Bake the shell for 10 minutes. Remove the paper and beans/beads and return to the oven for 10 more minutes. Cool.

Filling

> 1 cup sugar
> ½ cup cornstarch
> ⅛ teaspoon crushed kosher or Hawaiian salt
> 2¼ cups of milk
> 4 large egg yolks, slightly beaten
> 2 tablespoons unsalted butter
> 1½ teaspoons pure vanilla extract

1. Combine sugar, cornstarch, and salt in a medium saucepan. Stir in milk and egg yolks. Add butter and vanilla. Over medium heat, stir constantly until the mixture begins to thicken and starts to slowly bubble.
2. Turn heat to low and continue to stir mixture for 2 more minutes. Mixture will become very thick.
3. Pour into cooled pie crust and set aside.

Meringue Topping

> 4 large egg whites, room temperature
> 1 cup sugar
> ⅛ teaspoon cream of tartar
> ½ teaspoon pure vanilla extract

1. Combine egg whites, sugar, and cream of tartar in a heatproof bowl. Place over a simmering saucepan of water on medium heat. Stir until sugar is dissolved and mixture is warm to the touch.
2. Transfer bowl to counter and begin mixing with electric mixer on low speed until frothy. Beat at high speed for about 10 minutes or until stiff, glossy peaks form. Add vanilla and combine.
3. Spoon or pipe, decoratively, on top of pie. If using a spoon, drawn meringue up into little peaks using the back of a tablespoon. Return to oven for about 10 minutes or until meringue is golden brown.
4. Let pie cool to room temperature, then refrigerate for at least 4 hours or overnight.

Serves eight.

Garden Gathering

WHEN YOUR GARDEN is waking up after a dreary winter, why not welcome it with a garden gathering? When your garden is bursting with blossoms and crops at the halfway point of summer, why not say "thank you" with a garden gathering? When your garden is decelerating after it has bestowed its harvest in late autumn, why not bid it adieu—for now—with a garden gathering? Who isn't fond of showing off their garden during any season? One of the best ways I know to glory in the glow of your garden is to host a gathering with a feast made from items you grew in your garden.

What could be more satisfying than to prepare recipes with produce grown in your garden or found at your local farmers' market? Provide teas, cocktails, or flavored water. Pick flowers from your garden and place bouquets in vases on your table and near benches around your yard. If you're entertaining in the evening, run strings of tinkle lights in arbors, around trees, along garden paths, or hanging from umbrellas over your tables. I also enjoy placing votive candles either in paper bags or in clay pots along walking paths and on the tables. There are so many creative ways to generate a pleasant mood.

I will invite our guests to walk around the garden and pick heirloom cherry or yellow pear tomatoes directly from the vines. I also grow green and Concord grapes. Guests are thrilled to see clusters hanging under broad leaves, and I encourage them to pick one and taste. It's thrilling to see the grins on their faces as they savor the sugary sweetness that you don't encounter with the grapes you obtain at your grocer.

Another gathering that celebrates gardening is a spring plant share. As your perennials begin to emerge and need dividing, place the divisions in pots with labels for identification. Invite your friends, neighbors, and their friends. Choose a time and request that each visitor bring a plant to contribute to the plant share. Everyone is welcome to take what they want or need. Offer beverages, cookies, and confections. I also like to place gardening books on a table for reference and planning. Some guests at the plant share may not be familiar with the growing requirements, such as whether the plant needs sun or shade, how much space it should have, or how much water it needs. It's also satisfying to see photographs of what the plant will ultimately look like. It's a wonderful way to begin the spring season, have a gathering in your garden, and meet with like-minded gardeners.

SUGGESTED SELECTIONS FOR YOUR GARDEN GATHERING

- Champagne Cocktails
  - Mimosa
  - Bellini
- Rhubarb Tea
- Raspberry Cordial
- Strawberry-Onion Salad with Poppy Seed Dressing
- Cool Cucumber Salad
- Olive and Sun-Dried Tomato Spread
- Caramelized Onion Jam
- Onion-Dill Bread
- Spinach Pie
- My, Oh My, Mushroom Pie
- Strawberry-Rhubarb Cobbler
- Raspberry Muffins
- Blackberry Jam Bars

Champagne Cocktails

Mimosa

I have a couple of friends who prefer nonalcoholic drinks. Go ahead and substitute nonalcoholic champagne if you like. Remember, everyone is welcome at the table.

> Champagne, chilled
> Orange juice, freshly squeezed is best but ready-made is fine

1. Fill one-fourth of a champagne flute or wineglass with champagne.
2. Fill the rest of the flute or wineglass with orange juice. Garnish with a slice of orange.

⸔ Bellini

The Bellini was created in 1948 at Harry's Bar in Venice, Italy, by Giuseppe Cipriani, Harry's head bartender. Giuseppe had a fondness for the Italian white peach and labored a long time to develop the perfect cocktail that would use this fruit as a base. He eventually tried a simple recipe of pureed white peaches and prosecco (Italian sparkling wine). How lucky we are for his perseverance.

During a trip to Las Vegas, Nevada, in 2003, we celebrated my birthday. Our good friend Lorna Benson joined my partner, Chad, and me at Todd English's Olives located in the Bellagio Hotel. We were seated with a remarkable view of the fabulous Bellagio fountains. Lorna suggested that I try a Bellini to celebrate my birthday and begin the evening, along with a black truffle and foie gras hors d'oeuvre. I was instantly placed into a trance; I have never forgotten the wonderful blend of pureed peaches and fine champagne—at least until we traveled to Venice, Italy, where the Bellini was born, and the memory became clearer.

   White or regular peach puree, such as California white peach puree
   Italian sparkling wine or champagne, chilled

1. Fill champagne flute or wine glass ¼ full with white or regular peach puree.
2. Add Italian sparkling wine or champagne, slowly so as not to foam, to top of flute or glass. Stir gently to blend.

"If you have a garden and a library, you have everything you need."

—Marcus Tullius Cicero

⸙ Rhubarb Tea

10 stalks fresh rhubarb, chopped
8 cups water
½ cup sugar
Fresh spearmint
Rhubarb spears

1. In a stockpot, bring rhubarb and water to a boil. Reduce heat and simmer for 1 hour. Strain the liquid through a sieve lined with cheese-cloth into a pitcher. Add sugar and stir until sugar has dissolved. Place in refrigerator until well chilled.
2. Rub a spearmint leaf along the rim of each glass to brighten up the experience. Cut rhubarb stalks into thin spears. Place in glass with ice. Add spearmint garnish and serve.

Makes two quarts.

⸙ Raspberry Cordial

My grandmother made a raspberry cordial for the children. Of course, that recipe did not have the vodka added. You may make either version with or without vodka. This version is wonderful served in cordial glasses or mixed in chocolate mousse. It also is an alternative additive to my Chambord Cheesecake featured in the chapter titled "Gathering to Celebrate Our Unions." Try serving over ice cream on warm summer nights for an extra indulgence; your guests will be glad they were invited to your home. Thank you, Grandma, for giving me another recipe for raspberries.

2 cups sugar, preferably cane sugar
2 pints fresh ripe raspberries
1 quart good-quality vodka

1. In a 3-quart or larger container with a tight lid, place sugar, raspberries, and vodka. Gently stir to combine. The sugar will not dissolve. Eventually it will, and this will not affect the cordial. Place in a dark cool place such as a basement.
2. Each week for the next three months, open the container and stir mixture. When cordial is ready, strain through a sieve lined with cheesecloth into a decanter or decorative bottle.

⸙ Strawberry-Onion Salad with Poppy Seed Dressing

This mixture of sweet strawberries and strong red onion topped by a creamy poppy seed dressing is an event you and your guests will comment on throughout your gathering. These are tastes you would not usually associate as companions, but remember: everyone and everything are welcome at the Garden County table. I hope you will be as surprised and delighted as I was by this union.

    1 pint fresh strawberries
    1 medium red onion
    1 head romaine lettuce
    ¾ cup mayonnaise (regular, low-fat, or fat-free)
    ¼ cup milk (regular or vanilla soy)
    2 tablespoons white vinegar
    2 tablespoons poppy seeds
    ½ tablespoon sugar

1. Rinse and slice strawberries and set aside. Cut onion into julienne slices and set aside. Rinse lettuce and dry. Combine berries, onion, and lettuce in a salad bowl. Toss.
2. Create the dressing by mixing together mayonnaise, milk, vinegar, poppy seeds, and sugar. Whisk until well blended. Transfer dressing to a pouring vessel and serve salad.

Serves six.

✦ Cool Cucumber Salad

Could there be anything more satisfying than picking a cucumber right from the vine in your garden and creating an instant salad? This recipe is just that type of creation. It is refreshing and very simple to prepare. Make my Cool Cucumber Salad ahead of time, and then when the mood suits you, curl up in the shade under a tree with a good book or a transistor radio tuned to big band or jazz.

    4 medium cucumbers, peeled and sliced
    1 small white onion, julienned
    ⅔ cups sour cream (regular, low-fat, or fat-free)
    2 tablespoons fresh dill
    ¼ teaspoon freshly ground black pepper
    ⅛ teaspoon kosher or Hawaiian salt

Slice cucumbers and onion and place in serving bowl. Gently stir in sour cream, dill, pepper, and salt. Chill 1 hour before serving. Serve on bed of lettuce greens or by itself.

Serves six.

✦ Olive and Sun-Dried Tomato Spread

    12 medium sun-dried tomatoes (if packed in oil, rinsed and well
        drained), finely chopped
    8 ounces cream cheese (regular, low-fat, or fat-free)
    ¼ cup sour cream (regular, low-fat, or fat-free)
    ½ cup black olives, chopped
    ¼ cup red onion, chopped
    Kosher or Hawaiian salt and freshly ground black pepper
    Chives

1. In a bowl, rehydrate tomatoes by pouring boiling water over to cover them. Let stand about 15 minutes. Drain and dry between paper towels.

If using tomatoes packed in oil, rinse with warm water, drain, and dry between paper towels.

2. Blend cream cheese and sour cream until smooth.

3. Add tomatoes, olives, and onion. Season with salt and pepper to taste. Mix well. Cover and refrigerate for at least 1 hour before serving. Garnish with fresh chives. Serve with crackers and/or crudités.

ʄ Caramelized Onion Jam

Oh, how I adore this jam. On a slice of Onion-Dill Bread (see following recipe in this chapter), life stops the instant you bite into this intense luxury filled with joyful flavors. Even my vocabulary becomes larger than life at the thought of indulging. Try a few spoonfuls on roast beef or barbecued pork chops. It's heavenly.

2 tablespoons unsalted butter
4 large onions, preferably Vidalia, finely sliced
⅔ cup dark brown sugar, firmly packed
½ cup brown malt vinegar
1 teaspoon fresh rosemary, finely chopped

1. Melt butter in a large heavy-bottom skillet over medium heat. Add onions and gently cook until soft and lightly brown. Add sugar. Stir into onion mixture until sugar dissolves.

2. Lower heat to low and simmer, stirring frequently, until mixture becomes thick and caramelized. Blend in malt vinegar and continue to simmer for additional 5 minutes. Mixture will thicken. Remove from heat and stir in rosemary. Let cool before serving. May be stored in airtight container in the refrigerator for five days. Spread on Onion-Dill Bread, pita chips, or barbecued meats.

⸗ Onion-Dill Bread

4 teaspoons active dry yeast
2 cups lukewarm water, 105 degrees or lower
2 tablespoons sugar
7½ cups all-purpose flour, divided
1 small onion, preferably Vidalia
4 tablespoons vegetable or olive oil, divided
1 fresh bunch dill, chopped
2 large eggs, slightly beaten
½ cup cottage cheese, small curd
4 teaspoons kosher or Hawaiian salt
Milk

1. In a large mixing bowl, blend yeast, water, and sugar together. Let stand, covered, for 15 minutes. Stir in 3 cups of flour. Cover again and let rise in a warm place for 45 minutes.
2. While yeast–flour mixture is rising, cook onion in a skillet with 1 tablespoon oil until translucent. Set aside and let cool completely. Stir into yeast mixture.
3. Add dill, eggs, cottage cheese, salt, remaining oil, and flour.
4. Place mixing bowl under a mixer with a bread hook attachment; lightly coat bread hook with cooking spray. Begin to mix dough until too stiff to continue mixing.
5. Turn out dough onto a lightly floured surface. Knead until smooth and elastic. Place in an oiled bowl and cover. Let rise for about 1½ hours or until doubled in size.

"Bread feeds the body indeed, but the flowers also feed the soul."

—The Koran

---

6. Grease or use a Silpat liner on a large baking sheet. Slice the risen dough in half. Shape into two rounds and place on baking sheet. Cover with a cloth and let rise another 30 minutes in a warm place.

7. Preheat oven to 375 degrees. With a sharp knife, score tops of dough to resemble lattice work. Glaze with milk. Place rounds in oven and spray walls of oven with water. This will create steam to bake moister bread. (You may omit this step if you are uncomfortable with it as it will produce hot steam.) You may also place a pan of hot water in the oven while preheating to create steam. Bake for about 50 minutes or until browned. Another technique to tell whether bread is completely baked is to tap your finger on the bottom. If the sound is hollow, the bread is ready. Cool on a rack and enjoy with Caramelized Onion Jam.

⸙ Spinach Pie

Crust

1½ cups all-purpose flour
½ tablespoon sugar
½ teaspoon kosher or Hawaiian salt
¼ cup cold all-vegetable shortening, cut into small pieces
¼ cup cold unsalted butter, cut into small pieces
¼ cup cold water
1 large egg yolk and 1 teaspoon water for egg wash

1. All ingredients should be cold. Combine all the dry ingredients in a large mixing bowl. Add shortening and butter. Using a pastry blender, cut in the shortening and butter until the mixture resembles coarse meal.

2. Drop by drop, add the cold water. Mix in with the fingertips, not with the hands as the palms will warm the dough. Continue mixing in water until the dough begins to hold together without being sticky but not crumbly.

3. Place dough in plastic wrap. Fold over plastic wrap and press down to form a disk. This will make rolling out easier after chilling. Finish wrapping in plastic and place in the refrigerator for at least 1 hour.
4. Lightly spray a 9-inch pie plate with butter or vegetable cooking spray. Roll out dough and place in pie plate. Return to the refrigerator until filling is ready. Makes pastry for one 9-inch single-crust pie.

Filling

½ cup unsalted butter
3 cloves garlic, chopped
1 small onion, chopped
4 large eggs, slightly beaten
1½ cups milk (regular or vanilla soy)
1 cup shredded Swiss cheese (regular or reduced fat)
4 ounces feta cheese, crumbled
1 10-ounce package frozen chopped spinach, thawed and drained
1 small can mushrooms, drained
1 package dry vegetable soup mix
Salt and pepper to taste

1. Preheat oven to 375 degrees. In a heavy-bottom skillet, melt butter over medium heat. Cook garlic and onion until translucent and soft. Do not brown as garlic becomes bitter. Remove from heat and cool slightly.
2. In a large bowl combine garlic-onion mixture, eggs, milk, cheeses, spinach, mushrooms, and dry vegetable soup mix. Season with salt and pepper. Stir until well blended. Pour into unbaked pie crust.
3. Bake for 50 minutes or until a knife inserted in the center comes out clean. Allow to cool for 10 minutes before serving.

Serves eight.

My, Oh My, Mushroom Pie

This is one of my favorite pies. I choose from a variety of mushrooms, including button, cèpe/porcini, chanterelle, cremini, morel, oyster, shitake, and wood ear. The wider variety of mushrooms you use will create a wealth of flavors that is difficult to describe. Be creative. Some mushrooms may be dried and need to be reconstituted in water before cooking.

Crust

3 cups all-purpose flour
1 tablespoon sugar
1 teaspoon kosher or Hawaiian salt
½ cup cold all-vegetable shortening, cut into small pieces
½ cup cold unsalted butter, cut into small pieces
½ cup cold water
1 large egg yolk and 1 teaspoon water for egg wash

1. All ingredients should be cold. Combine all the dry ingredients in a large mixing bowl. Add shortening and butter. Using a pastry blender, cut in the shortening and butter until the mixture resembles coarse meal.
2. Drop by drop, add the cold water. Mix in with the fingertips, not with the hands as the palms will warm the dough. Continue mixing in water until the dough begins to hold together without being sticky but not crumbly.
3. Divide dough into two pieces and place each in plastic wrap. Fold over plastic wrap and press down to form a disk. This will make rolling out easier after chilling. Finish wrapping in plastic and place in the refrigerator for at least 1 hour.
4. Lightly spray a 9-inch pie plate with butter or vegetable cooking spray. Roll out dough and place in pie plate. Return to the refrigerator until filling is ready. Roll out top crust and cut slits in the top. Makes pastry for 9-inch double-crust pie.

Filling

4 medium onions, preferably Vidalia, finely chopped
4 tablespoons unsalted butter
3½ pounds assorted mushrooms, chopped
3 teaspoons fresh French or English thyme
¼ cup Marsala wine
Kosher or Hawaiian salt
Freshly ground black pepper
1 tablespoon all-purpose flour

1. In a large skillet over medium heat, melt the butter and cook the onions until translucent. Add mushrooms and thyme. Slowly cook until mushrooms reduce in size.
2. Just as the mushrooms release their juices, add the Marsala and cook until the liquid is reduced by half. Season with salt and pepper. Add the flour and stir to combine. The juices will begin to thicken. Remove from heat and cool completely before pouring into the crust.
3. Preheat the oven to 400 degrees. Remove prepared pie crust from the refrigerator. Brush inside of pie crust and edge with egg wash. This will "glue" the bottom and top crust together and prevent the filling from bubbling out through the sides. Add mushroom filling. Place top crust over filling and seal. Trim and create a decorative edge around your pie. Apply egg wash. Bake for 35 minutes, or until crust is golden. Serve immediately and garnish with mushrooms and springs of thyme.

Serves eight.

Strawberry-Rhubarb Cobbler

    1¼ cups sugar
    1½ teaspoons cinnamon
    3 tablespoons all-purpose flour
    1 teaspoon orange zest
    7 cups fresh or frozen strawberries, ¼-inch slices (if using frozen, thaw and drain well)
    7 cups fresh or frozen rhubarb, chopped (if using frozen, thaw and drain well)

1. Preheat oven to 400 degrees. Spray 13- × 9-inch baking dish with cooking spray.
2. Combine sugar, cinnamon, flour, and orange zest in a large bowl. Gently stir in the strawberries and rhubarb. Spoon mixture into baking dish and spread evenly. Place in oven and bake for 10 minutes. While cobbler is baking, prepare topping.

Topping

    1½ cups all-purpose flour
    3 tablespoons superfine baker's sugar
    1½ teaspoons baking powder
    ¼ teaspoon kosher or Hawaiian salt
    ½ tablespoon baking soda
    3 tablespoons margarine (regular, low-fat, or fat-free)
    1 cup buttermilk

1. Combine flour, sugar, baking powder, salt, and baking soda. Using a pastry blender, "cut in" margarine with the dry ingredients until it resembles coarse meal. Sir in buttermilk until it forms a soft dough.
2. Remove cobbler from oven. Spoon topping in mounds over hot cobbler filling. Return to oven for an additional 25 minutes or until topping is golden. Serve with ice cream or fresh whipped cream.

Serves eight to ten.

🖋 Raspberry Muffins

Raspberries are, in my opinion, the most extraordinary fruit. Try these muffins that Grandma used to bake, with a pat of butter and raspberry preserves spread on them for an extra treat. They are simply heavenly by themselves also.

Batter

> 1½ cups all-purpose flour
> ½ cup sugar
> 2 teaspoons baking powder
> ½ cup milk (regular or vanilla soy)
> ½ cup unsalted butter or margarine, melted
> 1 large egg, slightly beaten
> 1½ cups fresh raspberries

1. Preheat oven to 375 degrees. Spray with cooking spray, or line with paper cups, a 12-cup muffin pan. Set aside.
2. Combine flour, sugar, and baking powder in a bowl. Set aside.
3. In another bowl, combine milk, butter, and egg until well blended. Stir in flour mixture until moistened.
4. Spoon ½ the batter into muffin cups. Place raspberries on top of batter and top with remaining batter. Sprinkle with topping and bake for 25–30 minutes.

Topping

> ¼ cup pecans, chopped
> ¼ cup dark brown sugar
> ¼ cup all-purpose flour
> 2 tablespoons unsalted butter, melted

Mix all ingredients together until moistened and crumbly. Sprinkle on top of batter before baking.

Serves twelve.

🍳 Blackberry Jam Bars

Berries are nature's wonderful gift. I work to create as many treats as possible to feature berries in all their glory. Find a blackberry patch and pick your own. Locate a recipe for blackberry jam or find a good-quality jam at your local grocer. Better yet, if the idea of canning your own jam doesn't thrill you, visit your local farmers' market and purchase a jar of homemade blackberry jam. You can use any berry jam in this recipe, depending on what is available. Enjoy!

⅓ cup unsalted butter, room temperature
½ cup dark brown sugar, firmly packed
1 cup all-purpose flour
¼ teaspoon baking soda
¼ teaspoon kosher or Hawaiian salt
1 cup oats, old-fashioned
1 cup blackberry jam

1. Preheat oven to 400 degrees. Spray an 8-inch-square baking pan with cooking spray. Set aside.
2. In the bowl of an electric mixer fitted with a paddle attachment, cream butter and sugar on medium for 3 minutes or until pale yellow. Combine flour, soda, and salt. Set aside. Turn mixer on low and add dry ingredients slowly until incorporated into creamed mixture. Stir in, by hand, uncooked oats.
3. Spoon ½ the batter into the baking pan. Using your fingertips, spread evenly in pan and slightly up the sides. Add jam and spread ¼ inch from edge of batter. Add remaining batter and press firmly to cover completely. Bake for 30 minutes. Cool and cut into bars.

Serves eight to twelve.

Housewarming Gathering

*H*ELPING FRIENDS AND FAMILY move into a new home is both exhilarating and hard work. It is a new beginning for them. Whether someone is upgrading their home or a couple is sharing their first home together, a housewarming gathering will set aflame the warmth of any new dwelling. Here are ways to help the occupants move in and receive guests in their household without being overwhelmed.

I have created recipes that will assist the moving crew with all-day soups, "Joes," casseroles, and breads. There are even sugary confections to boost the morale of the group after hours of carrying furniture and belongings.

I like to cook a good deal of each item, especially soup, so that everyone can take something home afterward. I also provide a set of pint and quart mason jars with lids. I always bring my label maker and, for safety reasons, a new box of freshly washed jars and lids. At the end of the day, I invite the helpers to ladle their favorite soups into jars and label them to take home. Everyone is exhausted after a hard day moving, and there is no better gift than a meal to take with them.

Of course, not everyone can lift heavy furniture and boxes. Those are the people we seek out to help prepare foods. I like to encourage them to bring their favorite bread to go with soup or, better yet, bake their favorite loaf to contribute. So, not everyone needs a strong back. However, if you have ever baked a loaf of bread you understand that strong arms are required.

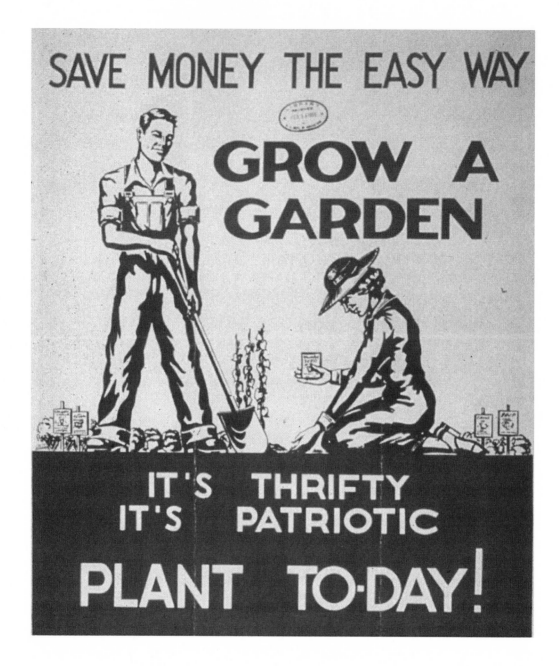

SUGGESTED SELECTIONS FOR YOUR
HOUSEWARMING GATHERING

- Peasant Bread
- Kaiser Rolls
- Herbed Pull-Aparts
- Banana Bread
- Chicken Noodle Soup
- Lasagna Soup
- Beer Cheese Soup
- Turkey Soup
- Vegetable Beef Soup
- Hitch and Go Turkey Joes
- Cheesy Potatoes
- County Fair Pound Cake
- Rum Sauce
- Almost Fat-Free Raspberry Almond Cheesecake

Peasant Bread

Grandma baked this bread for special occasions. It was considered "foreign" bread, so the occasion had to be special. The household receiving this bread always felt privileged. I remember Grandma giving this bread to someone at a potluck, and all the women in the kitchen uttering "oh" and "ah." I asked Grandma why everyone reacted that way. She explained that when she was small girl, food was given because people were very poor and had little money. Unique breads, cakes, or confections were made as gifts for occasions and gatherings. Taking extra time and using a recipe not normally made was something out of the ordinary.

I believe what made Grandma's breads so unique was her technique of using proofing baskets while the dough rose. This created raised markings that swirled around the bread and were covered in flour. This recipe can be made with or without a proofing basket. But, if you are unfamiliar with the concept, I do suggest examining one at your local cookware store. I have baked this bread for housewarmings and placed it unsliced in a basket lined with a checkered cloth, a roll of salami, large black olives, and a wedge of cheese.

2 cups warm (not hot) water, divided
1¼ teaspoons active dry yeast
1½ cups Sponge (see under The Basics)
6 to 7 cups bread flour
½ cup medium rye flour
1 tablespoon kosher or Hawaiian salt

1. In a large mixing bowl, combine ¼ cup water and yeast. Let stand for 15 minutes until yeast begins to produce small bubbles and turn foamy.
2. Add Sponge and, with a bread spoon, mix until incorporated. Add remaining water, 6 cups bread flour, rye flour, and salt. Continue mixing until dough becomes too difficult to stir. Turn out onto a lightly floured surface.
3. Knead dough and add flour, starting with a lesser amount, only as needed. Knead for 10 minutes or until the dough becomes smooth and elastic. Place dough in a bowl sprayed with cooking spray and cover with plastic wrap; cover bowl with a dishcloth. Let rise for about 3½ hours or until tripled in size.
4. Turn out dough onto a lightly floured surface. Split in half and, using hands, pull dough down in a circular motion creating either a rounded loaf or rectangular loaf or one of each. Set dough, rounded side down, in a proofing basket dusted with flour. Cover with a dishcloth and let rise until doubled in size, about 1 hour.
5. Preheat over to 425 degrees. Line a large baking pan with either a Silpat liner or a lightly floured piece of parchment paper.
6. Unload dough from baskets onto lined baking pan. Let rest for 15 minutes.
7. Place in oven and spray walls of oven with water. This will create steam to bake moister bread. (You may omit this step if you are un-

comfortable with it as it will produce hot steam.) You may also place a pan of hot water in the oven while preheating to create steam. Bake for 30 minutes or until browned. Another technique to tell whether bread is completely baked is to tap your finger on the bottom. If the sound is hollow, the bread is ready. Cool on a rack and enjoy.

⸕ Kaiser Rolls

These are grand rolls to take to any moving or housewarming party. I also like to construct a platter of deli meats such as country ham, roast beef, smoked turkey breast, and sliced salami, to which I add assorted cheeses, pickles, mustard, and relish. With such a platter you have the makings for some excellent sandwiches that are far better than any fast food from around the corner. The crew will be very happy that you arrived with this array of appetizing distractions.

    2 tablespoons active dry yeast
    2 cups warm water (not hot), divided
    4 tablespoons sugar, divided
    ⅓ cup vegetable or extra virgin olive oil
    2 teaspoons kosher or Hawaiian salt
    6 to 7 cups all-purpose flour
    1 large egg white and 2 teaspoons water for egg wash
    Sesame seeds
    Poppy seeds

1. In a large mixing bowl, combine yeast, ½ cup water, and 1 tablespoon sugar. Gently stir to help dissolve yeast and sugar. Let stand for 15 minutes.
2. Using a bread whisk or wooden spoon, stir in remaining water and sugar, oil, and salt. Add about 5 cups of flour and slowly mix until you have soft dough.

3. Turn out onto a lightly floured surface and begin kneading the dough until smooth and elastic, about 10 minutes. Add flour as needed to prevent dough being sticky. You should be able to press your finger anywhere in the dough and the surface will bounce back immediately.

4. Spray a clean large bowl with cooking spray. Place dough in bowl. Cover with a dishcloth and let rise until doubled in size, about 1 to 2 hours.

5. Punch dough down. With lightly floured hands, divide dough into 16 equal sized pieces. Shape each piece into a ball and place onto baking sheets lined with Silpat liners or sprayed with cooking spray. Cover with dish towels and let rise until doubled, about 1 hour.

6. Thirty minutes before dough is ready, preheat oven to 400 degrees. Place a pan of hot water on the lowest rack to create steam while rolls bake.

7. In a small bowl combine egg white and 2 teaspoons of water. Uncover rolls and brush with egg wash. Sprinkle half the rolls with sesame seeds and the other half with poppy seeds.

8. Using a sharp knife or bread tool, slice the tops of each roll in a criss-cross pattern. Bake for 20 minutes or until golden. Remove from oven and cool on racks.

Serves sixteen.

Herbed Pull-Aparts

I serve my Herbed Pull-Aparts with soups, roasted meats, and pasta dishes. The fragrance that fills your home will immediately tell your guests as they arrive that you've made them something spectacular.

> 2 tablespoons active dry yeast
> 8 cups all-purpose flour, divided
> 2 cups warm water
> ¾ cup vegetable or extra virgin olive oil
> ½ cup sugar
> 1 tablespoon kosher or Hawaiian salt

3 large eggs
1 cup parmesan cheese, grated
1 tablespoon fresh rosemary, finely chopped
1 tablespoon fresh sage, chopped
1 tablespoon fresh basil, chopped
1 tablespoon fresh thyme, chopped
1 large garlic clove, finely minced
¼ cup unsalted butter, melted

1. In a large mixing bowl, using a bread whisk or wooden spoon, combine yeast and 4 cups of flour.
2. Blend together water, oil, sugar, and salt. Add to flour mixture. Stir until well blended. Add eggs and beat with bread whisk or spoon until well incorporated. Using your hands, mix in remaining flour to make soft dough.
3. Turn out onto a lightly floured surface and begin kneading the dough until smooth and elastic, about 10 minutes. Add flour only as needed to prevent dough being sticky. You should be able to press your finger anywhere in the dough and the surface will bounce back immediately.
4. Spray a clean large bowl with cooking spray. Place dough in bowl. Cover with a dishcloth and let rise until doubled in size, about 1 to 2 hours.
5. In a bowl or shallow pan, combine cheese, rosemary, sage, basil, thyme, and garlic.
6. Punch dough down. With lightly floured hands, divide dough into three portions. Cover and let rest for 10 minutes. Divide each portion into eight equal sized pieces. Shape each piece into a ball and dip in melted butter. Roll each piece of dough in the cheese and herb mixture until completely coated. Place evenly in two 10-inch tube or bundt cake pans sprayed with cooking spray. Cover with dish towels and let rise until doubled, about 1 hour.
7. Thirty minutes before dough is ready, preheat oven to 375 degrees. Place a pan of hot water on the lowest rack to create steam while rolls bake.
8. Bake for 40 minutes until golden brown and tapping the top of the bread produces a hollow thud. Remove from pans and cool on racks.

Serves twenty-four.

Banana Bread

This terrific quick bread brings back fond memories of Grandma and Grandpa's farm. Grandma made this bread almost weekly as a treat for the farmhands. I enjoy making it for friends who are coping with stress at work or personal issues. I've also taken banana bread along when Chad and I have helped friends move. Of course, I usually make a couple of loaves so that everyone gets at least two pieces. I believe it is the use of almond extract that sends the sweetness meter over the top and makes this banana bread different from most other recipes.

1¾ cups all-purpose flour	⅓ cup all-vegetable shortening
2 teaspoons baking powder	⅔ cup sugar
¼ teaspoon baking soda	2 large eggs
½ teaspoon kosher or Hawaiian salt	1 teaspoon almond extract
	3 ripe bananas, mashed

1. Preheat oven to 350 degrees. Spray a loaf pan with cooking spray and set aside.
2. In a mixing bowl, sift together flour, baking powder, baking soda, and salt. Set aside.
3. In the bowl of an electric mixer with a paddle attachment, cream shortening until velvety. Gradually add sugar and continue to beat until light and fluffy.
4. Add eggs, one at a time, and blend well after each egg is added. Blend in almond extract.

"Your first job is to prepare the soil. The best tool for this is your neighbor's garden tiller. If your neighbor does not own a garden tiller, suggest that he buy one."

—DAVE BARRY

---

5. Alternately, add dry ingredients and mashed bananas in small amounts. Beat until each addition is well incorporated before adding more.

6. Pour into prepared pan and bake for 60 to 70 minutes or until a skewer inserted into the center comes out clean. Remove from oven and cool on a rack before serving.

⸗ Chicken Noodle Soup

I love preparing this soup on weekends during our Minnesota winters. The house is bursting with the aroma of chicken broth and fresh dill. It is a satisfying fragrance, and everyone who is home that day anticipates soup time. This is also a great soup for colds or flu. Whenever Chad, Heather, or I are ill, this is the cure-all. (It doesn't actually cure, but it does help you feel less miserable.) This is a soup that you can store in a quart mason jar and refrigerate for up to three days or share with friends and neighbors. I enjoy delivering a quart of it to any friend who is ill, along with a copy of his or her favorite magazine. It's my way of saying that I care.

3½ quarts chicken broth (see under The Basics)
3 carrots, chopped
2 celery stalks, chopped
8 ounces pasta (bow tie, penne, egg noodle, or any wide pasta),
    cooked and drained
2 cups chicken or turkey, cut into bite-size pieces (optional)
1½ teaspoons kosher or Hawaiian salt
2 teaspoons freshly ground black pepper
⅓ cup fresh dill, chopped
⅓ cup fresh Italian flat-leaf parsley, chopped
3 green onions with greens, chopped

1. In an 8-quart stockpot or large kettle over medium-high heat, combine broth, carrots, and celery. Simmer for 15 minutes, stirring occasionally.
2. Add cooked pasta, meat, salt, and pepper. Bring to a slow boil, stirring so that pasta does not scorch on bottom of pot. Reduce heat until bubbles are just rising to the top of the soup. Add dill, parsley, and green onions. Cover and simmer for 10 minutes stirring occasionally.
3. Remove from heat and serve.

Serves ten to twelve.

ⸯ Lasagna Soup

Whenever I have leftover Tuscan Tomato Sauce on hand, I cook up a pot of this soup. Of course, canned tomato sauce will work, but make sure you look for a good-quality sauce for the best flavor. If you have a chef's cooking torch available in your kitchen, use it to melt the cheese over the croutons and soup. The torch will brown the top of the cheese perfectly. This soup is easily poured into a crock pot and transported to any occasion. Let warm on low heat before serving.

 1 pound ground beef or ground turkey
 1 large onion, sliced
 2 large red bell peppers, seeded and diced
 2 large garlic cloves, minced
 4 cups water
 4 cups Tuscan Tomato Sauce (see under The Basics) or
     2 15-ounce cans tomato sauce
 2 cups lasagna noodles, broken into 1 inch pieces
 1 tablespoon dark brown sugar
 1 teaspoon fresh basil, chopped

"A garden is never so good as it will be next year."

—THOMAS COOPER

1 teaspoon fresh oregano, chopped

1½ teaspoons fresh Italian flat-leaf parsley, chopped

¼ teaspoon fresh ground black pepper

2 cups croutons

2 cups shredded mozzarella cheese (regular, low-fat, or fat-free)

1. In a heavy-bottom skillet over medium heat, cook meat until browned. Drain excess fat. Return to heat and add onion, peppers, and garlic. Cook until vegetables become tender.
2. Carefully pour meat and vegetable mixture in an 8-quart stockpot or large kettle. Add water and tomato sauce and stir until well blended.
3. Add pasta, brown sugar, basil, oregano, parsley, and pepper. Stir occasionally until boiling.
4. Turn heat to low, cover, and simmer until noodles become al dente or tender.
5. Serve in soup bowls and top with croutons and a sprinkling of shredded cheese.

Serves six to eight.

Beer Cheese Soup

This soup requires a strong arm because it must be stirred constantly to prevent scorching. If you are up to the challenge, the reward is a smooth, creamy soup that is extremely satisfying. I like to serve with Peasant Bread or Kaiser Rolls (see recipes in this chapter). Some of my guests have requested topping this soup with popcorn. I personally prefer no topping, only crusty breads for dunking.

¾ cup unsalted butter

3 carrots, finely chopped

2 celery stalks, finely chopped

1 large onion, finely chopped

1 cup all-purpose flour

8 cups chicken broth (see under The Basics)
½ teaspoon kosher or Hawaiian salt
¼ teaspoon freshly ground black pepper
2 pounds American pasteurized process cheese spread
    (regular or low-fat), diced
10 ounces sharp cheddar cheese, diced
2 12-ounce cans warm beer

1. In an 8-quart stockpot or large kettle, melt butter over medium heat. Add carrots, celery, and onion. Sauté until carrots and celery are tender and onions translucent.
2. Reduce heat to low and stir in flour. Continue cooking for 5 minutes, stirring constantly.
3. Add chicken broth, salt, and pepper. Increase heat to medium-high and bring to a boil, stirring constantly.
4. Reduce heat to low and add cheeses. Continue to stir slowly until the cheeses have melted. Remove from heat.
5. In small amounts, slowly pour beer into the soup and blend well. Serve immediately.

Serve ten to twelve.

Turkey Soup

Whenever I roast a turkey, I make this soup within the next couple of days. It is creamy and rich, but you can reduce the fat by using fat-free margarine and fat-free half-and-half. Nothing is lost in the conversion. If I don't have time to make this soup, I put the carcass in a storage bag and keep it frozen until I need it. I also store leftover soup in quart mason jars and refrigerate for up to three days. If I have too much soup, I'll drop off some for friends and neighbors to share. Add a loaf of crusty bread, and you'll have a feast.

1 turkey carcass

6 quarts water

1 cup unsalted butter

1 cup all-purpose flour

2 large onions, chopped

3 carrots, chopped

2 celery stalks, chopped

1 cup brown rice, uncooked

2 teaspoons kosher or Hawaiian salt

1 teaspoon freshly ground pepper

2 cups half-and-half
(regular or fat-free)

1. Place turkey carcass in an 8- or 12-quart stockpot or large kettle and add enough water to cover. Bring to a boil over medium-high heat. Cover and reduce heat until bubbles are just rising to the top of water. Simmer for 1 hour.

2. Remove carcass from broth and, when cool enough to handle, strip meat from the bones. Strain broth through a fine-mesh sieve or cheesecloth. Set meat and broth aside.

3. In an 8-quart stockpot, melt butter over medium-low heat. Add flour and, constantly stirring, cook for 5 minutes. Add onions, carrots, and celery. Continue to stir and cook an additional 10 minutes until vegetables are tender.

4. Add 3½ quarts of turkey broth, turkey meat, rice, salt, and pepper. Increase heat to medium-high and bring to a boil. Stir often as the rice tends to settle on the bottom of the stockpot and may scorch.

5. Reduce heat until bubbles are just rising to the top of the soup. Cover and simmer for 25 minutes or until rice is tender, stirring occasionally. Add half-and-half. Blend well and heat for 10 minutes.

Serves ten to twelve.

Vegetable Beef Soup

This is one of my favorite family recipes. Grandma would simmer the beef shanks until the meat fell off the bones. Depending on what was available in the garden, she would add green beans, peas, or corn freshly cut from the cob. Be creative with this soup and add your own favorite vegetables. Make sure that you simmer all vegetables until they are fork tender.

4 pounds beef shanks

2 quarts water

2 bay leaves

9 black, white, and green peppercorns (3 of each)

1 large onion, chopped

2 carrots, chopped

2 celery stalks, chopped

1 pound roma or vine-ripened tomatoes, seeded and chopped

1 teaspoon kosher or Hawaiian salt

¼ teaspoon freshly ground black pepper

1 teaspoon fresh marjoram

1 teaspoon fresh English or French thyme leaves

1. Place shanks in a large heavy-bottom saucepan and add water. Bring to a boil over medium-high heat. Add bay leaves and peppercorns. Reduce heat until bubbles are just rising to the top of the water. Cover and simmer for 2 hours.
2. Remove shanks from broth and, when shanks are cool enough to handle, remove meat. Cut into bite-size chunks. Strain broth through a fine-mesh sieve or cheesecloth. Skim any fat from the surface with a metal spoon.
3. Pour broth into an 8-quart stockpot or large kettle. Add meat, onion, carrots, celery, tomatoes, salt, pepper, marjoram, and thyme. Bring to a boil over medium-high heat. Reduce heat until bubbles are just rising to the top of the soup. Cover and simmer for 30 minutes or until vegetables are tender.

Serves eight to ten.

"The best stock a man can invest in, is the stock of a farm; the best shares are plow shares; and the best banks are the fertile banks of a rural stream; the more these are broken the better dividends they pay."

—H. W. Beecher

⨍ Hitch and Go Turkey Joes

My mother received this recipe as a child at old Duckworth #4, a one-room schoolhouse she attended in Grand Forks, North Dakota. She made this recipe for every occasion, especially birthday parties. Mom would use regular ground beef, but she didn't drain the excess fat. As I grew older and wiser about nutrition, I began draining the fat but I still was not satisfied with the result; I would develop stomachaches. There still was too much fat in the recipe. Then I tested the recipe with ground turkey. The switch did the trick and created a recipe that maintained the original flavor that I enjoyed but reduced the fat content significantly. Even now I consider these the best-tasting Turkey Joes I have ever eaten.

> 3 pounds ground beef or ground turkey
> 1 large yellow onion, chopped
> 1½ teaspoons Worcestershire Sauce
> ¼ teaspoon red pepper flakes
> 2 10-ounce cans chicken gumbo soup
> 1½ cups tomato ketchup (regular, light, or spicy)

1. Brown ground beef or turkey in a large kettle or 8-quart stockpot on medium-high. Add chopped onion and Worcestershire Sauce. Cook until onion is translucent. Drain off any excess fat.
2. Add red pepper flakes, chicken gumbo soup, and choice of ketchup. Stir to combine and simmer on low heat for 10 minutes.
3. Serve on sliced buns and sprinkle with shredded (regular, low-fat, or fat-free) cheddar cheese (optional).

Serves twenty-four (recipe may be condensed or doubled as needed).

Note: Once cooked, the mixture may be transferred to a crock pot and left on low heat to keep warm.

⸮ Cheesy Potatoes

Chad's mother, Diane Olson, shared this recipe with me several years ago. It is incredibly tasty and usually served at cold-weather holiday dinners. This is another wonderful dish to bring to a housewarming/moving party but can also made into a lower-fat dish by making a few simple choices. You can decide which you would prefer—full fat or low fat. Nothing is lost in the translation as far as taste is concerned. I made this for an Olson family dinner, and Chad's family, who had eaten this dish for many years, didn't realize that I had used fat-free ingredients because the taste remained the same. So we discovered that having a second or third helping of Cheesy Potatoes wasn't so bad after all.

¾ cup unsalted butter, divided
1 medium yellow onion, chopped
1 10-ounce can cream of chicken soup (regular or fat-free)
2 cups sour cream (regular, low-fat, or fat-free)
3 cups American pasteurized process cheese spread
    (regular or low-fat), diced
1 2-pound bag country-style hash brown potatoes
2 cups crushed corn flakes

1. Preheat oven to 350 degrees. Spray a 9- × 13-inch baking pan with nonstick cooking spray and set aside.
2. In a heavy-bottom sauce pan over medium-high heat, melt ½ cup unsalted butter. Add the chopped onion and soup. Turn heat to low and add sour cream and cheese spread. Stir until cheese has melted and all ingredients have combined.
3. Layer half the bag of hash brown potatoes in the prepared pan. Pour half the soup-cheese mixture over potatoes. Repeat with remaining hash browns and soup-cheese mixture.
4. Melt ¼ cup unsalted butter in a skillet over medium heat. Add crushed corn flakes. Stirring lightly, brown until sugar in cereal begins to caramelize. Remove when golden brown. Do not burn.
5. Sprinkle caramelized corn flakes over cheese potatoes.

6. Bake for 1 hour uncovered. Serve immediately or prepare one or two days ahead of dinner or party and store in the refrigerator in a tightly covered container. Great served warm or cold. Reheat in a 350 degree oven for 15 minutes.

Serves eight.

ƒ County Fair Pound Cake

I bake this pound cake in a variety of pans such as a decorative bundt pan in the shape of a rose, a mum, or a cathedral. You may also bake in a regular 10-inch tube pan. This is an old family recipe that was entered in many county fairs around the Red River Valley in the 1930s and 1940s.

   3 cups cake flour
   ½ teaspoon salt
   1 pound unsalted butter, room temperature
   1 pound sugar
   2 teaspoons pure vanilla extract
   6 large eggs, room temperature
   ½ cup buttermilk

1. Preheat oven to 325 degrees. Prepare a 10-inch regular tube or bundt-type cake pan with cooking spray.
2. Sift together the flour and salt. Set aside.
3. In the bowl of an electric mixer, beat the butter until creamy with the flat paddle on medium-high speed. Add the sugar gradually and continue to beat until light and fluffy. Add vanilla. Begin adding eggs one at a time, beating well after each addition and scraping down the bowl once or twice with a spatula.
4. Add the sifted dry ingredients in three batches, alternating with buttermilk. Combine well after each addition, scraping bowl as needed. After all the ingredients have been added, beat for about 2 minutes on medium speed to combine thoroughly. Do not overmix.

5. Scrape the batter into the prepared pan, smoothing the top with a spatula. Bake approximately 1 hour and 20 minutes, or until a toothpick or wooden skewer tests clean. The cake should be golden. Cool 20 minutes before gently removing from the pan. Place on a cake board or decorative cake plate and wrap with plastic wrap and foil to keep fresh and moist. Will keep at room temperature for up to five days. Freezes well for up to one month.

6. Sprinkle top of cake with confectioner's sugar (optional). Also spoon Rum Sauce (recipe follows) into center of cake or over individual slices.

ƒ Rum Sauce

I love this sauce with my County Fair Pound Cake, but it's also unbelievable spooned over ice cream, especially butter pecan. An unusual delight for a cold Sunday afternoon treat is spooning Rum Sauce over Grandma's Sticky Buns (see under Gathering at Mokihana on the Island of Kauai) and offering my guests thick hot chocolate for a beverage.

2¼ cups water, divided
½ teaspoon cornstarch
1 cup sugar
1 teaspoon ground cinnamon, preferably China Cassia
1 tablespoon unsalted butter
1 tablespoon dark rum

"Flowers in a city are like lipstick on a woman—it just makes you look better to have a little color."

—LADY BIRD JOHNSON

1. In a small bowl, combine ¼ cup water and cornstarch. Set aside.
2. In a heavy-bottom saucepan over medium heat, bring to a boil 2 cups water, sugar, cinnamon, and butter.
3. Add cornstarch mixture and stir until well blended. Continue to boil mixture, stirring constantly. Remove from heat and add rum. Blend well.
4. Spoon into center of cake baked in tube or bundt pan, on serving plates with slice of cake, or pour into decorative sauce boat for individual serving.

Almost Fat-Free Raspberry Almond Cheesecake

This recipe is another of my much-loved desserts because it uses my favorite berry, the raspberry. We have several raspberry canes in our garden. This was one of the main reasons I wanted to purchase our house and yard. We stood outside in the raspberry patch, discussing the specifics of the house with the owner. As we talked, we picked luscious red raspberries and filled our mouths. The taste was overwhelming, and I believe I had decided on buying the house before we made it back to our vehicle. The raspberries clinched the deal!

Recently, I made this cheesecake as a housewarming gift and set it on a clear glass pedestal cake stand. I gave the cake with the stand to the hostess as our gift to their new home. Consider baking a treat for a new home owner and presenting it on a cake stand or plate, or in a decorative pan for the recipient to keep. I added a jar of my homemade raspberry jam as an extra gift, which I also used to top this luscious cheesecake. You may substitute regular or low-fat items where fat-free items are suggested. The cheesecake will rise a bit higher with regular items, but it will taste the same.

1¾ cups graham cracker crumbs
1 cup sugar, divided
6 tablespoons fat-free margarine, softened
1½ pounds fat-free cream cheese

3 large eggs, room temperature
½ cup fat-free half-and-half
⅛ teaspoon kosher or Hawaiian salt
1 teaspoon almond extract
1 cup raspberry jam or preserves (regular or sugar-free)
½ cup finely silvered almonds

1. Preheat oven to 350 degrees. Wrap the outside and bottom of a 9-inch springform pan in a double layer of aluminum foil.
2. In the bowl of a food processor, combine graham crackers and ¼ cup sugar. Process to a fine crumb. Add fat-free margarine and process until margarine has been incorporated into crumb mixture. Press crumb mixture into bottom of pan. Place in a freezer until cheesecake mixture is ready to pour.
3. Beat cream cheese in the bowl of an electric mixer fitted with the paddle attachment; mix on medium speed until fluffy, about 3 minutes. With mixer on low speed, add ¾ cup sugar in a slow, steady stream. Add eggs, one at a time, mixing each until well combined. Mix in half-and-half, salt, and almond extract. Pour over chilled crust.
4. Set springform pan in a larger baking or roasting pan and place in oven. Slowly pour hot water halfway up the side of the cake pan. Bake for 70–80 minutes or until the center is almost set.
5. Cool on wire rack completely before refrigerating at least 6 hours or overnight. Run knife around edge of pan to loosen.
6. Spread jam or preserves evenly over the top of the cooled cheesecake. Sprinkle almonds decoratively over the jam or preserves.

Serves sixteen.

Picnic Gathering at the GLBT Pride Celebration

$\mathcal{E}$ACH YEAR I AWAIT the Twin Cities Gay, Lesbian, Bisexual, Transgender Pride Celebration at the end of June the same way a child anticipates Christmas. A lot of planning goes into choosing which events to attend, including parties at local clubs and the festival in Loring Park, which begins on Saturday. All of this is capped off by the Ashley Rukes GLBT Pride Parade on Sunday morning. The morning of the parade, I pack a picnic lunch.

We arrive early Sunday morning for the parade and find a great viewing spot on the main route along Hennepin Avenue to watch the floats, marching bands, cars filled with fabulously dressed people waving, and, my favorite, those marching for Parents, Families and Friends of Lesbians and Gays. My view is obstructed every year with tears of elation as I watch mothers, fathers, and family members proudly supporting their children, brothers, and sisters. Perhaps it is the loveliest vision of summer.

When we hear the thunderous motorcycle roar of Dykes on Bikes, we know that the parade is beginning and coming down the avenue. The parade lasts approximately three hours. And as the last float maneuvers its way to Loring Park, we grab our gear and follow it to the entrance of the park. We carry our lunch and all the booty we have collected from parade participants who gladly throw it to us. I'm very partial to lots of bead necklaces and Frisbees that I turn over and use as plates when I travel. (I throw them sometimes, too!)

Once we arrive at Loring Park, we find a grassy spot by the lake and have our picnic lunch. Afterward, we walk among the booths and entertainment. For me this is the official start of summer, but, more important, the community comes together to celebrate its diversity. There is no abhorrence or name-calling, and no self-righteous men and women denouncing who we are—just lots of rainbows, smiles, greasy food, and music. What could be better? More than 300,000 people come together to rejoice in life and all the diversity. One truly walks away with a joyful heart.

So prepare your picnic hamper, basket, or bag. I have used large festive gift bags with handles. Fill yours with plastic flatware and plates. Don't forget the napkins and a bag to collect the trash. Pack simple and light; it's going to be a long day. I've been on picnics where the host has gone "all out" with crystal goblets, fine china plates, and gourmet foods. It was exciting and a special way to picnic, but it was also a great deal of work for the host. If you decide on a grandiose picnic, you may want to line up help. However you decide to host your picnic gathering, don't forget to save a little room for the mini-donuts, corn dogs, and Hawaiian shaved ice sold at booths later in the day.

Tips for Your Successful Picnic

1. To keep your drinks chilled for your picnic, freeze them the night before. Not only will they stay cold the next day, they'll also help keep your food chilled in the picnic container.
2. Bring a colorful and comfortable blanket or tablecloth. I have two checkered tablecloths, one blue and one red. They provide a comfortable place to sit as well as a surface on which to serve your food.
3. To keep bees and wasps away from your picnic, place sprigs of fresh mint around your blanket or tablecloth. If you rub a sprig or accidentally sit on one, you will release its wonderful aroma. If fresh mint

"We're here, we're queer, let's eat!"

—JOHN MICHAEL LERMA

doesn't keep the bees and wasps away, put it in your drinks. Either way you can't lose.

4. Hot weather can spoil food quickly. Using your frozen drinks will keep your food well chilled, but store everything in an ice-filled cooler for added protection.

5. Throw away any food that has been out of the cooler for more than an hour, especially any food made with eggs or mayonnaise products.

6. Sometimes we decide on a whim to go on a picnic. Take the trouble out of packing. Have all these items already in your hamper, basket, or bag. All you need to add is food.

- Blanket or tablecloth
- Insect repellent
- Pocket radio or portable CD player
- Napkins
- Paper plates
- Plastic silverware
- Plastic serving utensils
- Plastic cups and wine glasses
- Corkscrew
- Condiments
- Wet wipes stored in a plastic bag for washing up
- Garbage bag—respect your parks by always cleaning up

SUGGESTED SELECTIONS FOR YOUR PICNIC GATHERING
AT THE GLBT PRIDE CELEBRATION

- "Slurries" in a Jar—Champagne with Frozen Fruits and Berries
- Melon Coolers
- Buttered Pecan Halves
- Eggs Stuffed with Crab Meat
- Cheese-Olive Balls
- Grandma's Iron Skillet Fried Chicken
- Garden County Potato Salad
- Broccoli-Raisin Salad
- Glorified Rice
- Roasted Garlic Bread
- Onion-Garlic Jam I ("Quick-Fix" Recipe)
- Onion-Garlic Jam II ("Old-Fashioned" Recipe)
- Assorted Cheeses That Travel Well

"Slurries" in a Jar—Champage with Frozen Fruits and Berries

On hot and humid summer days in Minnesota, I pack these icy pleasures for picnics, lying on a floatation device while bobbing around on Twin Lake, or as a simple respite from working in my garden. Naturally, you need to sip—not gulp. All things in moderation, and please be careful in or around water and when using gardening tools, especially ones that have sharp blades and rotate.

I love mason jars and use them in all my canning and preserving. With their secure tops, they make a natural choice for transporting drinks and food. You may use whatever you have handy, or perhaps you already have a favorite container for liquids. Enjoy and treat yourself to a reward of frozen fruit and fun.

Recipe for Champagne Slurry
(see under The Academy Awards Gathering)
Pint or quart mason jars with lids and screw bands

1. Place jars, lids, and bands in the freezer until ready to use.
2. Prepare recipe for Champagne Slurry
3. Spoon frozen fruit mixture into chilled jars and cover tightly with lids and bands. Leave at least ½-inch head space (space between liquid and top of jar) and return to freezer for at least ½ an hour.

Melon Coolers

In my universe there is nothing more invigorating than fresh melon, either chilled or at room temperature. This recipe creates either a slush-type drink, or you can substitute milk for the orange juice and produce a smoothie. If you decide to prepare either version for your pleasure trip, make it ahead and chill in your freezer for an hour before leaving. This will allow you to serve nicely chilled Melon Coolers during your outing. As the day wears on your coolers will remain slushy while you sip.

8 cups seeded watermelon, honeydew, or cantaloupe cut in
1-inch chunks
1 cup fresh mint leaves
1 cup water
½ cup orange juice, divided
or
½ cup milk (regular, skim, or vanilla soy), divided
Extra mint leaves for rubbing and garnish

1. Place cubed melon, in one layer, on a jelly roll or cookie sheet baking pan. Put in the freezer for 1 to 2 hours or until frozen.
2. Bring water to a boil. Place mint leaves in a heat-proof bowl. Pour boiling water over leaves, cover, and let steep for 15 minutes. Drain

and reserve mint liquid. Discard mint leaves. Refrigerate "mint tea" until cold—about 2 hours.

3. In blender, combine half the frozen melon chunks and half the mint tea. Add ¼ cup orange juice or milk. Blend on high until smooth but thick. Serve in festive glasses or chilled mason jars to transport for your picnic. Rub rim of glass with fresh mint to brighten the sipping experience. Garnish with melon balls on paper umbrellas and a sprig of fresh mint.

Serves eight.

Buttered Pecan Halves

Place a half-cup of these wonderful treats in a cellophane bag and tie it up with a ribbon. When you spread out your blanket or tablecloth and all your food is ready for your picnic gathering, offer each person at your gathering a packaged present. I like to offer my guests, whether at an outdoor gathering or during the winter holidays, a little gift they can enjoy immediately or later when they return home. It's like taking a part of the party home. You could attach a note card with something special written inside, such as, "By the time you read this, I'll still be smiling."

2 cups pecan halves	1 teaspoon garlic powder
½ cup unsalted butter	Kosher or Hawaiian salt

"Queer things happen in the garden in May. Little faces forgotten appear, and plants thought to be dead suddenly wave a green hand to confound you."

—W. E. JOHNS

1. In a heavy-bottom skillet, melt the butter over low heat. Add pecans and slowly cook until browned, stirring occasionally to keep from scorching.
2. Remove from heat and sprinkle with garlic powder and salt. Gently stir and let cool. Double recipe as necessary.

Serves four.

⨏ Eggs Stuffed with Crab Meat

This is my variation on deviled eggs. I call them crabby eggs: not as spiteful as deviled eggs but still eggs with attitude. It just wouldn't be a picnic without half an egg filled with something appetizing.

>   6 hard-boiled eggs
>   1 teaspoon ground mustard
>   ½ teaspoon kosher or Hawaiian salt
>   1 cup crab meat, flaked
>   1 cup celery, finely chopped
>   2 tablespoons Grandma's Sweet Cucumber Relish
>   (see under Festival of the Moonflower)
>   1 cup mayonnaise (regular, low-fat, or fat-free)
>   Black olives, sliced
>   Paprika

1. Cut cooled hard-boiled eggs in half and remove the cooked yolks. In a mixing bowl mash yolks with a fork. Add mustard, salt, crab meat, celery, relish, and mayonnaise. Chill in refrigerator for half an hour to let flavors develop.
2. Fill cooked egg whites with mixture using either a spoon or a pastry bag fitted with a decorative tip. Place on serving plate dressed with assorted greens. Top each filled egg with a slice of black olive and sprinkle with paprika.

Makes twelve.

Cheese-Olive Balls

Along with the Glorified Rice recipe in this chapter, this one seems to be in every grandmother's, great-aunt's, or cousin's recipe box. I adore this appetizer, and it travels well, especially on picnics. You can also make it ahead of time and freeze it. Prepare the balls, store them in freezer bags, and bake 20 minutes before serving. I like to poke a toothpick with colorful plastic on the end or, better yet, a paper umbrella through each one for serving. That makes it easier to dip them in honey mustard also. These are a festive appetizer for a festive occasion. And what is more festive than a gathering of friends? Bon appétit!

½ cup unsalted butter, softened
1 cup sharp cheddar cheese, grated
¼ teaspoon kosher or Hawaiian salt
⅛ teaspoon cayenne pepper
½ cup all-purpose flour
Dash Worcestershire sauce
Dash paprika
24 green olives, pimiento-stuffed and drained

1. Cream together butter and cheese. Add salt, pepper, flour, Worcestershire, and paprika. Blend well. Chill cheese dough for 20 minutes.
2. On a lightly floured surface, flatten the cheese dough and cut into 24 squares. Place an olive in the center of each piece of cheese dough. With hands dipped in flour, shape around olive. Set on an ungreased baking sheet. Chill for 1 hour.
3. Preheat oven to 400 degrees. Bake for 10 minutes or until lightly browned. Serve warm or at room temperature.

Makes twenty-four.

---

*"Wind chimes in your yard will serenade garden creatures . . .
squirrels, fairies and angels."*

—AUTHOR UNKNOWN

⸰ Grandma's Iron Skillet Fried Chicken

Yes, an iron skillet is named in the title because it is the ideal cooking utensil for frying the best chicken you have ever tasted. Grandma insisted on it when she cooked, and I travel with mine all over the United States. (I haven't tried taking it through customs yet!) This is the most requested of all recipes in my collection. I make it for picnics, bicycle rides, celebrations, and even Christmas Eve dinner. I hope you enjoy this special delight as much as my family and friends have.

2 quarts buttermilk

⅓ cup kosher salt

1 2-ounce bottle of hot
    pepper sauce

2 whole chickens—cut up
    or large variety pack

3 cups all-vegetable
    shortening

3 cups all-purpose flour

2 tablespoons baking powder

1 tablespoon ground
    black pepper

1½ teaspoons ground
    cayenne pepper

1 heaping tablespoon spice mixture

Spice Mixture

½ teaspoon salt

½ teaspoon pepper

½ teaspoon paprika

½ teaspoon thyme

½ teaspoon turmeric

½ teaspoon onion powder

½ teaspoon garlic powder

½ teaspoon superfine baker's sugar

1. Combine buttermilk, kosher salt, and hot pepper sauce in large nonreactive bowl. After washing chicken, swirl chicken pieces in the liquid. Cover with plastic wrap and refrigerate for at least 4 hours or (best) overnight.
2. Heat vegetable shortening in a cast iron skillet over medium heat. Shortening should not come to a rolling boil.
3. Combine flour, baking powder, black and cayenne pepper, and spice mixture in a doubled large brown paper sack. Shake to blend thoroughly. One piece at a time, place the chicken in the bag and shake until well coated.

4. Place each piece of chicken in skillet. Do not crowd or chicken will not fry thoroughly. Fry until the coating is a dark golden color on the bottom—about 15 minutes. Using tongs, turn chicken and cook another 15 minutes until dark golden.
5. Drain on platter covered with several layers of paper towels or use layers of brown paper bags on the kitchen counter.
6. After frying a couple of pieces, use a slotted spoon to remove any bits of flour coating left in the skillet and discard.
7. To keep fried chicken warm, place on a baking sheet in a 200-degree oven.

Serves eight to ten.

Note: Unfortunately, the buttermilk and hot pepper sauce marinade must be discarded. Spice mixture, however, can be stored in a tightly covered jar or plastic bag for future use.

Garden County Potato Salad

Grandma made this potato salad when the potatoes were just harvested. She cooked the red potato slices with 1 tablespoon freshly squeezed lemon juice so that the potatoes would not yellow during the boiling. While the potatoes were boiling, Grandma and I would grab our wooden harvest baskets and go out to the garden to see what else was ready to pick and add to the potato salad. If we didn't have green onions, Grandma would use yellow onions. If the carrots were not ready, she would shred broccoli or cauliflower. You get the idea. If you don't have a garden in your backyard, look for what's in season at your local farmers' market.

This is a great potato salad to bring to any picnic gathering. For easy storage and transportation, use an empty, clean ice cream bucket to mix, chill, and serve the potato salad. It's a great way to recycle.

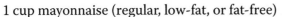

1 cup mayonnaise (regular, low-fat, or fat-free)

½ cup sour cream (regular, low-fat, or fat-free)

3 tablespoons yellow mustard (I prefer Dijon mustard, but you can make it Grandma's way. It just depends on your taste.)

1 teaspoon sugar

1 teaspoon kosher or Hawaiian salt

1 teaspoon garlic, minced

½ teaspoon ground white pepper, Indonesia coarse grind if available

3 pounds red potatoes, unpeeled

3 large hard-boiled eggs, chopped

½ cup green onions, chopped with greens

½ cup Italian flat-leaf parsley, chopped

½ cup carrots, shredded

2 tablespoons fresh dill, chopped

1. Bring a large pot of water to a boil over medium-high heat. Salt the water and add a little lemon juice to keep the potatoes white. Slice potatoes thinly. Set aside.

2. In large mixing bowl, combine mayonnaise, sour cream, mustard, sugar, salt, garlic, and pepper. Set aside to let flavors blend while potatoes are boiling.

3. When water begins to boil, add potatoes. Bring to a boil again. Turn heat to low and simmer until potatoes are just tender. You do not want them soft or crumbling. Remove from heat and rinse with cool water. Drain and set aside.

   Here's a short cut: During the last 10 minutes of simmering your potatoes, lay the eggs on top of the potatoes. Slowly push them down into the simmering water and hard-boil while the potatoes are finishing their cooking.

4. Add eggs, onions, parsley, carrots, and dill to large mixing bowl with mayonnaise mixture and blend well. Add potatoes and gently turn until well coated. Place in a covered container and chill for several hours.

Serves eight to ten.

Broccoli-Raisin Salad

½ cup mayonnaise (regular, low-fat, or fat-free)
2 tablespoons white vinegar
2 tablespoons sugar
2 teaspoons milk (regular or vanilla soy)
½ pound bacon (regular or turkey)
2 bunches broccoli, washed and drained
½ cup green onions, chopped with greens
½ cup golden raisins
½ cup sunflower seeds, toasted

1. In a large bowl, blend mayonnaise, vinegar, sugar, and milk. Set aside.
2. Cook bacon until crisp. Drain on a paper towel. When cool crumble and set aside.
3. Cut broccoli into bite-size pieces and add to bowl with dressing. Add onions, raisins, bacon, and sunflower seeds. Stir until well mixed.

Serves six to eight.

Glorified Rice

Is there anyone whose grandmother, great-aunt, or third cousin once removed didn't have a version of this recipe? It is a pretty standard recipe, but I enjoy this dish and think it's a delightful old-fashioned addition to any picnic—especially appropriate for any pride festival. Immediately upon tasting this family favorite, conversations will begin about family gatherings or reunions. My grandmother brought her recipe up a notch

"What is a weed? A plant whose virtues have not yet been discovered."

—RALPH WALDO EMERSON

by adding multicolored miniature marshmallows. That was a pretty daring move in the Red River Valley during the 1960s. Enjoy the festivities!

1 cup white rice, cooked
1 cup heavy whipping cream
½ cup sugar
½ teaspoon pure vanilla extract
1½ cups pineapple, diced (fresh or canned)
2 tablespoons maraschino cherries, chopped
⅓ cup miniature marshmallows

1. Prepare rice; drain, rinse, and cool to room temperature.
2. In a mixing bowl, whip cream until thickened. Add sugar and vanilla until blended. Fold in pineapple, cherries, and marshmallows.
3. Add cooled rice and gently stir until well mixed. Refrigerate for at least 2 hours before serving.

Serves six.

Roasted Garlic Bread

1 garlic bulb separated and roasted (see instructions in step 1, below)
2 tablespoons extra virgin olive oil, divided
4 cups bread flour
2 tablespoons sugar
1 teaspoon kosher or Hawaiian salt
1 tablespoon or one packet active dry yeast
1½ cups water
Milk

"Of course . . . people go both ways . . ."

—SCARECROW TO DOROTHY ON THE YELLOW BRICK ROAD

---

1. Heat oven to 350 degrees. Line a shallow baking pan or pie plate with aluminum foil. Set aside. Separate cloves and carefully peel outer skin from each individual clove. Spread cloves evenly on foil-lined baking pan. Drizzle with 1 tablespoon olive oil. Securely wrap the foil and bake for 45 minutes. Let cool before adding to bread dough.
2. Using an electric mixer fitted with a bread hook, spray bread hook with cooking spray. Sift flour into mixing bowl and stir in sugar, salt, and yeast.
3. Add water and remaining olive oil. Mix on medium until mixer can no longer knead. Pour out dough on lightly floured surface. Knead dough until elastic. Place in an oiled bowl, cover with a dishcloth, and let rise until doubled in size.
4. Punch dough down. Stretch dough on lightly floured surface and place roasted garlic cloves on dough. Lightly knead to incorporate cloves into the dough. Return to bowl, cover, and let rise a second time for 1 hour.
5. Preheat oven to 450 degrees. Divide dough in half and shape into round loaves. Place on baking sheet lined with parchment paper. Let rise 30 minutes. Brush rounded loaves with milk. Bake for 25 minutes until brown and tapping on the bottom of bread produces a hollow thud.

Makes two 1-pound loaves. Serve with assorted cheeses or Onion-Garlic Jam (see recipes I and II below).

Onion-Garlic Jam I

This is my grandmother's "quick-fix" Onion-Garlic Jam. She would offer this for gifts, and it could be cooked up in a fraction of the time it took for her regular Onion-Garlic Jam (see following recipe). This jam needs to be refrigerated immediately and may be stored up to two months in the refrigerator. Onion-Garlic Jam is phenomenal on roast pork or beef. Also slather a large spoonful on my Roasted Garlic Bread, Peasant Bread, or Onion-Dill Bread.

10 garlic cloves, finely chopped
¼ cup onion, finely chopped
1 cup rice vinegar
¼ cup cane sugar
4½ pint jars apple jelly

1. In a large heavy-bottom saucepan, combine garlic, onion, vinegar, and sugar. Dissolve sugar over low heat, stirring occasionally. Raise heat to medium-high. Bring mixture to a boil, stirring to prevent scorching. Continue to boil mixture until liquid has reduced by half.
2. Add apple jelly and stir to combine. Bring all ingredients to a boil, gently stirring, until the jelly melts. Ladle Onion-Garlic Jam into clean half-pint jars. Leave ¼ inch headspace, wipe rims, and seal with lids. Let cool on a rack. Store in refrigerator for up to two months.

Makes four to five half-pint jars.

ʄ Onion-Garlic Jam II

When Vidalia onions are ready each spring, you'll find me in my kitchen preparing several batches of this wonderful old-fashioned jam. I treasure it as one of my most prized gems in the pantry. When Chad and I take a road trip to somewhere like Decorah, Iowa, I bring along freshly baked bread and a jar of my Onion-Garlic Jam. While Chad drives, I slice pieces of bread and spread the jam on the bread. We listen to music, chatter, and enjoy this wonderful picnic/road trip pleasure. Try it at your next parade, festival, or impromptu picnic by the lake.

"In the spring, at the end of the day, you should smell like dirt."

—MARGARET ATWOOD

---

2 tablespoons unsalted butter
2 tablespoons extra virgin olive oil
3 pounds, about 5½ cups, onions, finely chopped, preferably Vidalia
10 garlic cloves, finely chopped
4 cups cane sugar
2 cups good-quality white wine
1 tablespoon freshly squeezed lemon juice
2 3-ounce pouches of liquid pectin

1. In a large heavy-bottom saucepan or stockpot, heat butter and oil over low heat. Once the butter has melted, add the onions and cook until translucent. Do not brown. Add garlic and stir gently for about 5 minutes. Do not let garlic brown as it will become bitter. If there is a good deal of liquid after cooking the onions, drain before adding the remaining ingredients.

2. Add sugar, wine, and lemon juice, continuing to cook over low heat until the sugar has dissolved. Raise the heat to medium-high and bring mixture to a full boil. Stir constantly to prevent scorching. Once mixture begins to boil, add both pouches of pectin. Bring mixture back to a rolling boil, continuing to stir. Boil for 1 minute starting from the time that you cannot stop the mixture from boiling, no matter how much you stir. Remove from heat.

3. Ladle Onion-Garlic Jam into half-pint jars that have been prepared per manufacturer's instructions. Leave ¼ inch headspace. After a couple of minutes, use a plastic knife or utensil to gently stir the jam to help evenly distribute the onion and garlic. Wipe the rims and seal with lids, also prepared per manufacturer's instructions. Before processing, let jam mixture cool slightly. Process sealed jars for 10 minutes using the hot-water-bath method. If you use pint jars, process for 15 minutes. As with all canning and preserving, review USDA instructions (see Web address under The Basics, "Homemade Canned Roma Tomatoes") and follow all safety measures.

⸕ Assorted Cheeses That Travel Well

Asiago: Asiago is named for the northern Italian village in which it was created. Serve with apples, pears, red or green grapes, figs, crusty breads, and pasta.

Brie: Brie ripens from the outside in, rather than the inside out. Serve heated or at room temperature with green apples, strawberries, pears, melons, grapes, sun-dried tomatoes, toasted walnuts and pecans, crackers, croissants, and crusty breads.

Gorgonzola: If you wanted to make Gorgonzola like they did in the olden days, you'd have to leave it in a cave for over a year. Serve with pears, raisins, walnuts, sweet crackers, and fruit breads

Gruyère: More than 1,000 years ago, Gruyères was the Swiss word for "forest," as well as the name of a small town in the Swiss Alps. Serve with red apples, melon, dates, figs, hazelnuts, and walnuts.

Havarti: American-made Havarti can trace its roots to the Havarti farm in Denmark. Select one of the many popular flavored varieties of Havarti—garlic and herb, jalapeño, dill, or caraway. I purchase Dill Havarti at the St. Paul Farmers' Market weekly. Serve with pears, red grapes, roasted red peppers, olives, almonds, rye bread, and bread sticks.

Parmesan/Parmigiano: Born in Parma, Italy, parmesan has a long aging period, anywhere from fourteen months to four years. Eat it on its own with a bottle of wine rather than using it as grated topping. But grating it for pasta dishes is not a bad thing, either. My best friend, Dan Kenward, and his partner, Ron Iverson, were our guests one evening. I served a pasta dish and a large chunk of Parmesan with a grater. I handed it to Dan. "It doesn't come in a green container?" he asked quizzically. Serve with pears, red grapes, raisins, figs, walnuts, and hearty breads.

Pecorino: Pecorino is the name given to all Italian cheeses made from sheep's milk. Pecorino Romano is one of the oldest and most versatile of these cheeses. My favorite cheese in the entire world, pecorino has a salty quality along with the aged goodness of parmesan. Serve with pears, red grapes, raisins, figs, walnuts, and hearty breads.

Cheese Tips

- Cheese is more flavorful at room temperature. Let it stand for a half hour before serving.
- Bring to room temperature only what you need. Leave the rest wrapped tightly in the refrigerator.
- Cheese should be stored at temperatures between 35 degrees and 40 degrees Fahrenheit in the original wrapping or container, waxed paper, transparent wrap, foil, plastic bags, or tightly covered containers.
- Cheese will continue to ripen, no matter how carefully it is stored. Hard cheeses will generally keep for several months, whereas softer cheeses will keep from one to three weeks after opening, if stored in an airtight container.
- Shredded cheese is more prone to mold because it has more exposed surface area. Try to use shredded cheese within a few days.
- Aromatic cheeses (blue, etc.) should be stored in airtight containers.
- I have the good fortune to own a home food vacuum. I store large blocks of cheddar, Swiss, parmesan, and pecorino vacuum packaged in the refrigerator for up to eight months. I can reopen and repackage daily if necessary (for most cheese normal storage life would only be up to two weeks in the cheese's original retail packaging or regular storage bags). This is one device that effectively has solved any issues with cheese that I have mentioned.

Gathering to Celebrate Our Unions

THE LONGER WE'RE IN RELATIONSHIPS, the harder it is to remember ways of pursuing your partner. What I mean is that you know your partner, and what will make him or her happy, better than anyone and may end up taking the relationship for granted. Chad and I enjoy taking each other on "dates" and spending time alone together. When we celebrate a major holiday such as Valentine's Day or our anniversary, we usually end up at an expensive restaurant or crowded club. I began looking at different ways to celebrate our union.

One of the best examples of finding a different way to celebrate was Valentine's Day 2005, when Chad and I attended a "love tour" at the Minnesota Zoo. We arrived and were greeted with champagne and hors d'oeuvre. We then had our photo taken together before embarking on an exotic animal encounter tour that lasted an hour. During the tour the guides discussed the mating habits of the animals while Chad and I sipped champagne. After our tour we walked to dinner along a hallway that featured information and games such as "pin the body part on the animal" or "the mating quiz." It was so much fun.

Dinner was spectacular. We sat in the aquarium area with tide pools full of starfish and sea urchins. There were exhibits and two floor-to-ceiling aquariums with sharks, eels, and a variety of exotic sea life. One aquarium had five dolphins that often swam within our view. The meal was fabulous, but I couldn't take my eyes off the dolphins or my partner. What an extraordinary evening, and it cost no more than dining in a crowded restaurant would have.

Don't wait for Valentine's Day or an anniversary to celebrate your coming together. Try some of these ideas and recipes to tell the person you love how truly you adore him or her. Keep it simple and keep your love alive.

Love Detour

Invite your partner along on a routine outing such as grocery shopping, dropping clothes off at the cleaners, or any simple chore. Before, during, or after your chores, take a detour to someplace else. When was the last time the two of you took a couple of hours just to talk and drive out to the country or the lake? Maybe you live close to a favorite coffee shop or café that you both enjoy but haven't been to lately. If you're very clever, you can pack a hamper with your partner's favorite snacks and take him or her to a little park to simply enjoy the sun and each other.

How Do I Love Thee? Let Me Count . . .

Create a list of reasons why you love your partner. You don't need to have a degree in English, be a poet, or print using calligraphy. Come up with as many reasons as you can. Take some time and list everything. Pick a number—perhaps fifty reasons or one hundred. Start with why you fell for your partner in the first place and build from there. I knew someone who used yellow sticky notes for this project. While his partner was sleeping, he lined the hallway to the bathroom with more than a hundred notes. He wrote items like "I loved the way you walked up and said hello that first night" and "I love you because you share your popcorn at movies" and "I love you a little more each time you call me from work to say you love me." The list is endless and very special. It will tell the person you love just how much you care, but it will also help you recall why you love this person.

Playtime

When was the last time you stopped at a playground and played on the swings or monkey bars? Now that you're an adult you can do this whenever you want, but how long has it been? Recapture a sense of spur-of-the-moment fun by doing silly things you haven't done in years. Visit an amusement park or a county fair. Ride the merry-go-round and the Ferris wheel. Share some cotton candy. Play hide-and-seek or tag in your own backyard. Whatever you do, if you get the blood pumping, you'll probably end your playtime in an entirely different way than you did when you were eight years old.

Invitation to Dance

How often do you hear, "We used to go dancing all the time"? Turn off the television and put on some special music that you can slow-dance to. Make this part of a special dinner that you cook before your partner comes home. Better yet, get dressed up and go out to your "old favorite" dance club, order a glass of wine, and dance for an hour. Then go home and enjoy each other's company. You don't need to stay out all night, but just one hour will bring back wonderful memories of what you both "used to do."

Private Servant

Purchase a card that holds dollar bills. Create a gift card or currency that allows the bearer to a private servant for one night. The terms must be that you will do absolutely anything he or she asks, without complaint. No matter how much you dislike shopping, playing video games, or whatever your partner asks, the best gifts come with no strings attached. This will show how much you value your partner, and it might expose you to some things that are more fun than you thought they would be.

"Won't you come into the garden? I would like my roses to see you."

—Richard Brinsley Sheridan

SUGGESTED SELECTIONS FOR GATHERING TO
CELEBRATE OUR UNIONS

- Take Them to Paradise Theme
    - Macadamia Nut Crusted Coconut Shrimp
    - Kalua Pig
    - Shoyu Chicken
    - Coconut Pudding with Blackberries
    - Exotic Fruit Platter
- Cinnamon Raisin Bread
- Garlic Elation Pie
- Garden-Fresh Garlic Pesto Pizza
- Almost Fat-Free Chocolate Truffle Cheesecake
- Raspberry Sauce
- Chocolate Chip Cookies
- Blackberry Margaritas
- Chambord Cheesecake

Take Them to Paradise Theme

What could be more fun than cooking a special lunch or dinner with a theme for your partner? I stopped by a local party store and found Hawaiian-themed plates, cups, a tablecloth, serving dishes, and a music CD. When Chad arrived home from work, I started the music and served a Hawaiian-themed dinner. I also set out the photo albums from our recent trip to Kauai. After dinner, I played our trip DVD while we enjoyed a Hawaiian-themed dessert.

⸱ Macadamia Nut Crusted Coconut Shrimp

Extra virgin olive oil
½ cup all-purpose flour
1 pound shrimp, deveined with tails on
½ cup canned coconut milk (regular or light)
½ cup macadamia nuts, crushed

1. Preheat oven to 400 degrees. Coat an 8- × 8-inch or 9-inch round baking dish with oil. Set aside.
2. Arrange, in separate bowls, flour, coconut milk, and macadamia nuts.
3. Coat shrimp in flour, then dip in coconut milk. Roll in macadamia nuts. Lay in baking dish. Repeat with until all shrimp are coated.
4. Bake for 15 to 20 minutes or until shrimp are cooked through and coating is toasted. Serve on a bed of banana leaves with lemon and lime wedges.

Serves four.

⸱ Kalua Pig

1 fresh pineapple
3 pounds pork shoulder
2 cups apple cider (pressed, not from concentrate)
1 teaspoon liquid smoke

1. Trim rough rind from around pineapple. Retain top of pineapple for platter decoration. Cut pineapple in thick slices. Refrigerate all but three slices.
2. Place pork shoulder in a large slow cooker or crock pot. Pour cider and liquid smoke over pork. Place pineapple slices around sides of pork. Cover and turn on low. Cook slowly for 8 to 10 hours.
3. Remove pork from cooker/pot and shred meat. Serve on a platter surrounded by pineapple slices and pineapple top.

Shoyu Chicken

    1 fresh pineapple, trimmed
    1 cup soy sauce (regular or light)
    ¼ cup dark brown sugar
    ¼ cup white wine
    1 teaspoon ground ginger
    2 large garlic cloves, minced
    3 pounds boneless, skinless chicken thighs cut into bite-size pieces

1. Slice trimmed pineapple. Crush enough pineapple to yield 1 cup. Refrigerate remaining pineapple to serve with chicken.
2. In a large heavy-bottom saucepan or kettle, combine crushed pineapple, soy sauce, sugar, wine, and ginger. Over medium-high heat, bring to a boil. Reduce heat to low and add garlic and chicken.
3. Simmer slowly for 1½ hours until chicken is fork tender.
4. Serve on a bed of palm fronds surrounded by pineapple slices.

Serves eight to ten.

Coconut Pudding with Blackberries

    1 14-ounce can coconut milk (regular or light)
    1½ cups water
    ⅔ cup sugar
    ⅔ cup cornstarch
    1 pint fresh blackberries

1. In a heavy-bottom saucepan over medium heat, combine coconut milk, water, sugar, and cornstarch. Stir to combine. Continue to stir until mixture thickens.
2. Reduce heat to low and, stirring constantly, cook for another 10 minutes. Do not stop stirring or mixture could burn or scorch.

3. Pour into an 8- × 8-inch baking pan. Chill in the refrigerator for at least 2 hours or until completely set. Cut into diamond shapes.
4. Serve topped with blackberries.

Note: If blackberries are out of season, top with crushed pineapple, sliced mango, or sliced kiwi.

Serves eight.

⸕ Exotic Fruit Platter

I enjoy searching the local farmers' market for exotic produce. I visit each store with a list in mind of what I would like to serve. For my exotic platter I wanted items we had dined on while on our Hawaiian vacation. I found many of the fruits, but I needed to travel to three markets in the Twin Cities. Don't limit yourself. Try a variety of fruits and even vegetables for your partner or guests. During a luau party, I placed index cards by each fruit with its name. Next to the platter I set a large book listing exotic fruits of the world that included beautiful photographs. There is no need for a fruit dip. Invite your partner or guest to suck the sweet juice out of sugar cane.

> 3 star fruit, sliced ½ inch thick
> Baby bananas (choose the ones that look overripe and black—
> they're the sweetest)
> 2 mangos, sliced
> 2 papaya, sliced in half
> 3 kiwi, sliced thick
> Pineapple, quartered (provide a knife so that guests can cut chunks
> out of the quarters)
> Rambutans (canned and stuffed with pineapple if fresh are not
> available)
> Coconut chunks
> Sugar cane

Serves ten to twelve.

⸙ Cinnamon Raisin Bread

Surprise the one you love on a weekday morning before work or on Sunday morning with the newspaper and a warm loaf of my Cinnamon Raisin Bread. Cut a big slice with warm glaze still dripping and top it with room-temperature butter or fat-free margarine. Of course, this exquisite morning would not be perfect without a freshly brewed cup of Italian roast coffee.

> 1 tablespoon dry active yeast
> 1¼ cups warm water
> 2 tablespoons honey
> 2 tablespoons margarine (regular, low-fat, or fat-free)
> 1 teaspoon kosher or Hawaiian salt
> 3 cups flour
> 1 tablespoon cinnamon (preferably China cassia)
> 1 cup dark raisins
> ½ cup confectioner's sugar
> 1 tablespoon milk (regular or vanilla soy)
> ½ teaspoon pure vanilla extract

1. In a large mixing bowl, dissolve yeast in water. Stir in honey and let rest for 5 minutes.
2. Add margarine, salt, and flour. With bread whisk or spoon, mix until well blended. Cover with dish towel and let rise until doubled, about 1 hour.
3. Punch dough down. Gently fold in cinnamon and raisins. Cover and let rise until doubled again, about 1 hour.
4. Preheat over to 375 degrees. Spray a loaf pan with cooking spray. Transfer dough to prepared loaf pan. Bake for 40–50 minutes or until golden brown. Remove from oven and cool on rack.
5. Before bread is completely cool, prepare glaze. In a small bowl combine confectioner's sugar, milk, and vanilla. Whisk until smooth. Place a baking pan under cooling rack. Pour glaze over Cinnamon Bread. Slice and serve.

Garlic for Lovers!

Garlic may not be ideal for your first date, but it can have major benefits for a couple's love life. Eating garlic actually widens arteries and improves blood flow. Let's just say that ancient Greek and Italian women fed garlic to their men as an early form of Viagra.

It's also a way to say "I want you around to grow old with." Heart specialists have discovered the health benefits of garlic. It can help prevent heart problems, and may help fight cancer and the MRSA "superbug," a drug-resistant infection. Dr. Joerg Gruenwald, a research scientist at Berlin University, said: "We have evidence of how garlic works in heart disease where the arteries are widened so that they reduce the chance of a heart attack. A lot of men with heart disease will have impotence but not realize poor circulation and narrowing of the arteries in the groin is to blame."

Other benefits have been indicated in research published by gynecologists from Chelsea and Westminster Hospital, London. They found that mothers-to-be can boost the birth weight of small babies by taking garlic to help increase the blood flow to the uterus. It was also discovered that garlic can cut the risk of preeclampsia, a condition in which increased blood pressure threatens pregnant women and unborn babies.

Besides the health benefits, garlic adds so much to any dish. Try the next two recipes. After dinner you and your partner can take turns brushing each other's teeth for something new to do together. After eating all that garlic who knows where it may lead?

"The air of Provence was particularly perfumed by the refined essence of this mystically attractive bulb."

—ALEXANDRE DUMAS

⸓ Garlic Elation Pie

Crust

1½ cups all-purpose flour
½ tablespoon sugar
½ teaspoon kosher or Hawaiian salt
¼ cup cold all-vegetable shortening, cut into small pieces
¼ cup cold unsalted butter, cut into small pieces
¼ cup cold water
1 large egg yolk and 1 teaspoon water for egg wash

1. All ingredients should be cold. Combine all the dry ingredients in a large mixing bowl. Add shortening and butter. Using a pastry blender, cut in the shortening and butter until the mixture resembles coarse meal.
2. Drop by drop, add the cold water. Mix in with the fingertips, not with the hands as the palms will warm the dough. Continue mixing in water until the dough begins to hold together without being sticky but not crumbly.
3. Place dough in plastic wrap. Fold over plastic wrap and press down to form a disk. This will make rolling out easier after chilling. Finish wrapping in plastic and place in the refrigerator for at least 1 hour.
4. Lightly spray a 9-inch pie plate with butter or vegetable cooking spray. Roll out dough and place in pie plate. Return to the refrigerator until filling is ready. Makes pastry for 9-inch single-crust pie.

Filling

½ cup unsalted butter
4 medium sweet onions, preferably Vidalia, sliced
2 or 3 large bulbs of garlic (⅓ to ½ pound), cloves peeled
    and thinly sliced
3 large eggs, slightly beaten
½ cup milk (regular, low-fat, or vanilla soy)

¼ teaspoon freshly ground pepper
1 cup freshly grated cheddar cheese (regular, low-fat, or fat-free)
1 cup freshly grated Pecorino Romano cheese
Kosher or Hawaiian salt for sprinkling

1. Preheat oven to 350 degrees. In a heavy-bottom skillet, over medium heat, melt butter. Add onions and garlic and sauté until translucent. Stir continuously and do not brown or garlic will become bitter. Remove from heat and let cool slightly.
2. In a medium mixing bowl, combine eggs, milk, pepper, and cheeses. Set aside.
3. Evenly distribute the sautéed onion and garlic mixture on the bottom of the prepared pie crust. Pour the egg and cheese mixture over the onions and garlic. Sprinkle with salt.
4. Bake for 35 minutes or until set and a skewer inserted in the center comes out clean. Remove from oven and let cool for 15 minutes on a rack before serving.

Serves eight.

✿ Garden-Fresh Garlic Pesto Pizza

1 12-ounce room temperature pizza dough (see under The Basics)
1 cup Basil Pesto (see under The Basics)
½ cup freshly grated Parmigiano-Reggiano cheese
¼ cup freshly grated Pecorino Romano cheese
1 bulb garlic, cloves peeled and thinly sliced
Fresh basil leaves, about 8, washed and dried
1 teaspoon good-quality extra virgin olive oil

1. Preheat oven to 450 degrees. If using homemade pizza dough, stretch room temperature dough into a thin round crust and place on a corn-meal-dusted pizza pan, parchment paper, or baking sheet. Do not use a rolling pin as this will push gases out of dough.

2. Add basil pesto and spread evenly. Grate cheeses over basil pesto. Evenly distribute garlic slices 5 minutes before end of baking time and continue to bake. Do not add basil leaves until after pizza comes out of oven or they will turn black.

3. Slide pizza into the hot oven and bake for 10 to 15 minutes. Baking times will depend on thickness of crust and amount of toppings.

4. Transfer to a cutting board and place fresh basil leaves on top of the baked cheeses. Brush edge of crust with olive oil to add shine and flavor.

Serves eight.

And Now, Sweets for the Sweethearts

ƒ Almost Fat-Free Chocolate Truffle Cheesecake

2004 Winner, Third Place Ghirardelli Chocolate Championship, Minnesota State Fair

My original recipe used regular dairy ingredients and was topped with chocolate butter cream frosting. It was a delicious cake, but I wanted to try something that retained the taste while reducing the fat by 90 percent. On the Weight Watchers Flex Plan, this recipe was reduced from 18 points per slice to 3 points per slice. Bake this cheesecake for someone you love and you both can enjoy it without any guilt. Using regular dairy products will result in a cheesecake that bakes higher, but using fat-free ingredients will not diminish the taste.

"No one is indifferent to garlic. People either love it or hate it, and most good cooks seem to belong in the first group."

—FAYE LEVY

1½ cups finely ground chocolate graham crackers

1⅛ cups sugar, divided

¼ cup margarine (regular, low-fat, or fat-free), melted

¼ cup semisweet chocolate chips

¼ cup half-and-half (regular or fat-free)

24 ounces cream cheese (regular, low-fat, or fat-free),
    room temperature

⅓ cup Dutch processed cocoa

3 large eggs

1 teaspoon pure vanilla extract

1. Heat over to 350 degrees. Wrap the outside and bottom of a 9-inch springform pan in a double layer of aluminum foil.

2. In the bowl of a food processor, combine chocolate graham crackers and ⅛ cup sugar. Process to a fine crumb. Add margarine and process until margarine has been incorporated into crumb mixture. Press ground mixture into bottom of pan. Place in a freezer until cheesecake mixture is ready to pour.

3. In a double boiler or microwave, melt chocolate chips. Stir in half-and-half and mix well. Set aside. Put cream cheese in the bowl of an electric mixer fitted with the paddle attachment; mix on medium speed until fluffy, about 3 minutes. With mixer on low speed, add remaining cup of sugar in a slow, steady stream. Add cocoa and beat well. Add eggs, one at a time, mixing each until combined. Stir vanilla extract and chocolate chip mixture into cream cheese batter until just blended. Pour over crust.

4. Set cake pan inside a larger baking or roasting pan and place in oven. Slowly pour hot water halfway up the side of the springform pan. Bake for 70–80 minutes or until the center is almost set.

5. Cool on wire rack completely before refrigerating at least 6 hours or overnight. Run knife around edge of pan to loosen.

Serves sixteen.

Raspberry Sauce

Here is a sauce that I make continually when my raspberries are in season. I pour over pancakes, chocolate chip cookies, my Chocolate Truffle Cheesecake, Chambord Cheesecake, and County Fair Pound Cake. Try it over ice cream or a warm brownie. You're only limited by your imagination.

½ cup sugar
½ cup water
2 cups fresh raspberries

1. In a heavy-bottom saucepan over medium heat, bring sugar and water to a boil, stirring occasionally. Reduce heat to low and simmer until sugar is completely dissolved.
2. Remove from heat. Cool to room temperature.
3. In a blender or food processor, combine sugar mixture and raspberries. Process until smooth. Strain through a fine mesh sieve or strainer. Use the back of a spoon to push juice through if needed. Discard solids. Store in jars for up to one week in the refrigerator.

Makes about two cups.

"A small garden, figs, a little cheese, and along with this, three or four good friends—such was luxury to Epicurus."

—FRIEDRICH NIETZSCHE

✦ Chocolate Chip Cookies

My grandmother made these cookies by hand. I would assist with the stirring, and I used to think my arm would break off. Grandma had a giant ceramic bowl and thick wooden spoon. One day I was baking bread and using my standing mixer. As I watched the bread hook kneading the dough, it occurred to me that I could use this machine to mix Grandma's chocolate chip cookie recipe. I tried it and it was a success.

This is one of my favorite cookie recipes. I've made large cookie cakes and decorated them with my Buttercream Frosting (see under The Basics) or smeared with a heated jar of River Chocolate Company chocolate sauce—any flavor—that I purchase at the St. Paul Farmers' Market or over the Internet. River Chocolate Company is dedicated to producing the finest chocolate sauces in the world. The company uses many single-plantation chocolates, organic sugar, and local organic cream and butter that are flavored with organic and natural extracts and essences from around the world and from local farms. This chocolate is unbelievable, and so are the owners, Allen Whitney and Deirdre Davis, whom I met years ago at the St. Paul Farmers' Market. Visit River Chocolate Company's Web site (www.riverchocolate.com) to order their extraordinary creations. I also like to serve these cookies warm to my partner with a scoop of vanilla ice cream and drizzle with my Raspberry Sauce and/or warm River Chocolate Company chocolate sauce.

2 cups unsalted butter	4 cups all-purpose flour
2 cups cane sugar	1 teaspoon kosher or Hawaiian salt
2 cups dark brown sugar	2 teaspoons baking powder
4 large eggs	2 teaspoons baking soda
2 teaspoons pure vanilla extract	2 12-ounce packages semisweet chocolate chips
5 cups old-fashioned oats	2 cups pecans, chopped (optional)

1. Preheat oven to 375 degrees. Spray baking pan with cooking spray. Set aside.
2. In the bowl of an electric mixer with a paddle attachment, cream butter and sugars. Add eggs and vanilla.

3. In a food processor, grind oats finely. Add to butter and egg mixture. Blend in flour, salt, baking powder, and baking soda.
4. Change paddle attachment to the bread hook attachment. Add chocolate chips and pecans. Mix on medium speed until well blended.
5. Roll dough into balls and set on baking pan. Bake for 8–10 minutes. Watch carefully so that cookies do not burn.
6. You also may bake on large cookie pans and decorate in place of a specialty cake or freeze dough balls in storage bags. Remove from freezer and bake in preheated oven for 10 minutes.

Depending on cookie size, makes seven to ten dozen cookies.

Blackberry Margaritas

2 cups canned blackberries with syrup
¼ cup white tequila
2 tablespoons orange liqueur, more for dipping rim of glasses
¼ cup freshly squeezed lime juice
2 cups crushed ice
Vanilla sugar

1. In a blender, combine blackberries and syrup with tequila. Blend for 10 seconds.
2. Add orange liqueur, lime juice, and ice. Blend until a smooth slush.
3. Dip rim of glasses in orange liqueur and vanilla sugar. Pour margaritas in glasses.

Serves two.

"So plant your own garden and decorate your own soul, instead of waiting for someone to bring you flowers."

—AUTHOR UNKNOWN

ƒ Chambord Cheesecake

I call Chambord liqueur the nectar of the gods. There is no greater gift than to receive this French black raspberry liqueur with its deep purple color in a bottle resembling a royal orb. Since its discovery by Louis XIV in 1685, Chambord has been known as the Liqueur Royale de France. With that idea in mind, I decided to create this cheesecake.

Heat a jar of River Chocolate Company Raspberry Chocolate Sauce and spread some on a dessert plate. Place a slice of Chambord Cheesecake on the plate and then drizzle my Raspberry Sauce in a crisscross pattern over the top. Place a few precious fresh raspberries on the side. This is true love, so serve to the one you love.

> 1½ cups finely ground chocolate graham crackers
> ¼ cup sugar
> ¼ cup unsalted butter or margarine (regular, low-fat, or fat-free), melted
> 16 ounces cream cheese (regular, low-fat, or fat-free)
> ⅓ cup sugar
> 3 large eggs
> ¼ cup Raspberry Cordial (see under Garden Gathering) or Chambord liqueur
> 1 teaspoon freshly squeezed lemon juice
> 2 cups sour cream (regular, low-fat, or fat-free)
> 2 teaspoons confectioner's sugar
> 1 tablespoon Chambord liqueur or Raspberry Cordial

1. Heat oven to 350 degrees. Wrap the outside and bottom of a 9-inch springform pan in a double layer of aluminum foil.
2. In the bowl of a food processor, combine chocolate graham crackers and sugar. Process to a fine crumb. Add butter or margarine and process until margarine has been incorporated into crumb mixture. Press ground mixture onto bottom of pan. Place in freezer until cheesecake mixture is ready to pour.
3. Beat cream cheese in the bowl of an electric mixer fitted with the paddle attachment; mix on medium speed until fluffy, about 3 minutes.

With mixer on low speed, add sugar in a slow, steady stream. Beat until light. Add eggs, one at a time, mixing each until combined. Blend in Raspberry Cordial/Chambord liqueur and lemon juice. Pour over crust.

4. Set cake pan inside a larger baking or roasting pan and place in oven. Slowly pour hot water halfway up the side of the springform pan. Bake for 60–70 minutes or until the center is almost set. Remove from oven and let rest for 15 minutes. Increase oven temperature to 450 degrees.

5. In a mixing bowl, combine sour cream, confectioner's sugar, and tablespoon of Chambord liqueur or Raspberry Cordial. Spread evenly over cheesecake. Return cheesecake to oven and bake for 5–7 minutes or until topping is set.

6. Cool on wire rack completely before refrigerating, at least 6 hours or overnight. Run knife around edge of pan to loosen.

Serves sixteen.

Gathering for a Backyard Barbecue

A BARBECUE IS THE ULTIMATE GATHERING because it starts with your backyard. I consider this an extension of our home, another "room," and it is one of my favorite areas of our home. In addition to an Italian four-season fountain in the center of our herb garden, we have a purple wisteria tree, strawberry beds surrounding the birdbath, Concord and green grapes scrambling up arbors with clusters of their round fruit hanging like pudgy wind chimes greeting all who wander underneath. We grow raspberry bushes that produce two harvests during the summer, and several heirloom tomato plants tied to tall support posts. I invite our guests to pick whatever is ripe and ready. It's wonderful to witness the expressions on their faces as they sample their first truly fresh blueberry or cherry tomato that likens the sun as if it had burst in your mouth. This is summer in our backyard.

I have an old "boom box" radio from the early 1990s that still works. I set it among the ostrich ferns and tune it to a local station that plays big band tunes from the 1940s and 1950s—Frank Sinatra, Doris Day, Glenn Miller. The mood is set and the party begins. All that is missing are the cocktails with paper umbrellas. Don't forget to make yourself one before delivering the serving tray to your guests.

This is the largest chapter in the book because I believe that a barbecue gathering is the largest gathering you can offer your guests. There are so many wonderful ways to prepare food. Your entertaining space can be decorated to suit your frame of mind: lights strung about the garden and backyard, music, garden architecture, water in pools, fountains, or barrels, and several interesting ways to present and display your food. The themes you can choose are infinite.

Before You Begin . . .

1. **Plan ahead and allow plenty of time.**

    I always harp on this topic, but it will make your life so much more pleasant. Create a list of recipes you want to make. Make sure you have all the ingredients. If someone asks to bring something, let them! I actually feel left out when I'm told that I don't need to bring anything. I like to cook, and it's my way of helping out. Prepare some dishes ahead of time, perhaps the night before. Make sure your list includes plates, cups, utensils, and condiments. Most important, don't rush. When have you ever had a guest who was in a hurry at a barbecue? If you find one, just pour them another mint julep!

2. **Keep it clean.**

    Maybe I'm a clean freak, but I cannot tolerate a grubby barbecue. I am usually asked to lend a hand in the cooking department by grilling the vegetables and meats. However, I have been asked to cook succulent meats on some of the most horrific grill grates. It's impossible to stop the burned-on charred chunks of last month's barbecue from attaching themselves to the fresh meats. I treat my barbecue like I do my good-quality stockpots, cast iron skillets, or carbon steel wok. A grill is a cooking utensil. Keep it covered when not in use. Scrape and brush the grill grate and rinse it with water. Before you preheat your barbecue, spray the grill grate with a cooking spray to prevent foods from sticking. Not only will your barbecue last longer, your food will not taste like last summer's hot dogs.

3. **Make sure you have good-quality tools for cooking.**

    Just as you take pride in the tools you have in your kitchen, take that pride into your backyard and study what you have hanging on the sides of your grill. How long have they been hanging there? Did you wash them after the last use? If you can answer these simple questions, you're on the right track. If you have no idea, I would say wash them thoroughly or go shopping. Find a good-quality grill set that includes a wide spatula, long sturdy tongs, a basting brush, and a long-handled fork. Also, pick up a grill brush, meat thermometer, and oven thermometer. Having reliable meat and oven thermometers will take the guesswork out of making sure your foods are cooked properly.

4. **What's with the sauce?**

   My father would slather chicken with barbecue sauce the minute he placed the chicken on the grill. This created chicken that was burned to a crisp—and I mean crisp. Our hamburgers and steaks were prepared the same way. I would spend the first five minutes of my meal peeling off the top layer of my food before eating it. I was admonished by my parents with the comment, "You're taking off the best part." I think good cooking sometimes skips a generation. Cook your meats first and then add the sauce. Approximately 5 to 10 minutes before your meats are completely cooked, add the sauce. This will prevent burning and allow the flavors of the sauce to cook into the meats. Letting your meats marinate overnight is another way to add flavor. I pour my sauce into a large two-cup bowl. This accommodates the wider barbecue basting brush to make basting your meats easier.

5. **Keep the H_2O handy.**

   As fat drips onto the coals or the element covering a gas burner, flames can leap up and get out of control. I keep a spray bottle of water turned on stream spray near my barbecue. This will douse the flames if they get too high and prevent your foods from scorching. Spray a stream of water at the base of the flame to put it out quickly. If this does not control the high flame, use baking soda to extinguish the flames. Having these two items nearby can prevent an unpleasant event while barbecuing.

SUGGESTED SELECTIONS FOR YOUR BACKYARD BARBECUE

- Barbecued Chicken Drummies or Wings
- Savoy Cabbage Slaw with Pesto Dressing
- Roasted Fresh Corn on the Cob
    - Corn on the Cob Essentials
- Corn and Roma Tomato Pasta Salad
- Cherry Tomato Pie
- Grilled Vegetables
- Hobo Onions
- Hobo Potatoes
- Potato Fritters
- Cornbread with Honey
- Kabobs
- Pulled Pork
- Blue Cheese–Stuffed Hamburgers
- Summer Stew (Barbecue Stew)
- Grandma's Ham Biscuits
- Lemon-Dill Salmon Steaks
- Grilled Pineapple
- Exotic Fruits Skewers
- Champagne Raspberry Parfait
- Lemon-Lime Cheesecake

⸮ Barbecued Chicken Drummies or Wings

This is one of Chad's and our friend Lorna Benson's favorite recipes that I have made for years. I tasted something very close decades ago in a restaurant called The Bronze Boot when I lived in Grand Forks, North Dakota. I was at a company dinner for Ruettell's men's clothing store, where I worked part-time while attending the University of North Dakota. They served these fantastic chicken wings that were salty and sweet and coated with a dark glaze. When I asked for the recipe, I was politely turned down. I toiled for months, trying to create the same taste that had thrilled me. Fortunately, Grandma had a similar recipe in one of her cookbooks, and I worked until I got it right. At least, it tastes just as good as I remember. Have this one ready when your guests arrive. I only get to have one or two pieces because the guests devour them. This recipe is dedicated to Chad and Lorna.

> 3½ to 4 pounds of chicken drumsticks or wings
> Kosher or Hawaiian salt
> Freshly ground black pepper
> 1 cup dark brown sugar
> 1 cup sherry cooking wine
> ½ teaspoon ground mustard
> 1¼ cups good quality soy sauce
> 3 large garlic cloves, minced

1. Preheat oven or barbecue to 350 degrees. In a large 13- × 9-inch baking pan (or make a foil pouch if baking in barbecue), arrange chicken drumsticks or wings in a single layer. Sprinkle salt and pepper over chicken and bake for 30 minutes turning halfway through.
2. In a heavy-bottom saucepan over medium heat, combine sugar, sherry, mustard, soy sauce, and garlic. Bring to a boil and remove from heat.
3. Pour sauce over chicken and return to oven or barbecue. Bake for another hour, turning chicken every 15 minutes.

Serves six to eight.

Savoy Cabbage Slaw with Pesto Dressing

I am always looking for different ways to use my basil from the garden. I vacuum-pack several bags of frozen pesto that has first been frozen in ice cube trays. You can use one cube or several cubes at a time when you want it. Our Minnesota winter is filled with pesto dishes all season long. You would never know it's snowing outside.

I prefer savoy cabbage, but you may use your favorite. I enjoy the buttery-nutty taste of savoy and use it for all my dishes requiring cabbage.

2 cups mayonnaise (regular, low-fat, or fat-free)
2 tablespoons Basil Pesto (see under The Basics)
1 large garlic clove, minced
1 teaspoon kosher or Hawaiian salt
1 teaspoon freshly ground black pepper
3 large carrots, shredded or cut into matchsticks
4 green onions, thinly sliced with greens
1 head of savoy cabbage, shredded
Italian flat-leaf parsley
Sicilian or regular basil leaves

1. In a large mixing bowl, combine mayonnaise and pesto. Whisk together until well blended. Add garlic, salt, and pepper. Set aside to let flavors mellow.
2. Using a food processor or knife, shred or cut carrots into matchsticks. Slice green onions and shred the cabbage, but leave in a few large strips and chunks.
3. Add carrots, onions, and cabbage to pesto dressing. Toss until vegetables are well coated. Cover and chill at least 1 hour. Before serving, sprinkle top of salad with a handful of parsley and basil leaves.

Serves eight to ten.

⸎ Roasted Fresh Corn on the Cob

This recipe both roasts and steams corn on the cob. The flavor is unbelievable served with herbed butter and Hawaiian salt. You may need to plan accordingly and offer each guest two cobs, because one is never enough!

Please read my Corn on the Cob Essentials on the following page. Corn on the cob is one of my favorite indulgences. If I am in Hawaii or Florida during the winter months, or anywhere tropical, the first thing I look for is corn on the cob. I grew up picking it fresh from our garden and putting it immediately into the pot. Today, I still try and grow my own in our tiny backyard. It has been a test of wills because the raccoons and squirrels enjoy fresh corn on the cob as much as I do. Fortunately, I have won that test for a couple of years. It's such a treat to walk into my garden, pick a golden ear of corn, and cook it right away.

> 1 dozen ears fresh corn
> Water
> Herbed or regular unsalted butter or margarine
>   (regular, low-fat, or fat-free)
> Hawaiian salt

1. Carefully pull back corn husks but do not remove from bottom stalk. Remove corn silk and discard. Pull husks back over corn and tie with a long husk or cooking twine.
2. Place prepared corn cobs in a large stockpot or kettle. Cover with cold water and let stand for 1 hour before placing on the hot grill.
3. Drain corn cobs and place on hot grill, turning every 10 to 15 minutes. Some of the husks may become charred—that's all right as long

---

"Let us be grateful to people who make us happy; they are the charming gardeners who make our souls blossom."

—MARCEL PROUST

as they do not start on fire. If husks catch fire, spray with water bottle and move from direct fire area.

4. Corn cobs are ready when husks are dry and begin to pull away from top of cob, usually around 45 minutes in a low- to medium-temperature barbecue. If using high heat, move to higher warming racks or to edges of grill for slow cooking.

5. Remove from heat and serve by pulling back husks and using the stalk as a handle. Slather with butter or margarine and sprinkle with salt. Enjoy!

Serves twelve unless your guests want more than one!

Corn on the Cob Essentials

When buying fresh corn, remember that it has been converting sweet-tasting sugars to starch from the moment it was picked off the stalk. Plan accordingly to purchase, cook, and serve it on the same day the corn was picked or as close to that day as possible. That is why I prefer corn from the farmers' market. I even ask the grower when the corn was picked. The luxury of the St. Paul Farmers' Market is that all produce must be grown within fifty miles of St. Paul. This guarantees the freshest corn and produce because it did not spend much time on a truck getting into town.

What to Look For

First, ask questions of the grower, such as when the corn was picked and what types of corn they are offering. Pick up each ear that you intend to purchase and weigh it in your hand. You want corn with substance. Look at the silk sticking out of the top of the ear. Corn silk should always be golden, full, and somewhat sticky. The more silk you see means more kernels of corn on your cob. The husk should appear deep green and not be turning brown or have black spots. I pull back the husk on each ear of corn that I plan to purchase and check the color of the kernels. You should not see black spots or gaps. That could mean a European corn borer—an insect that feeds on the corn plant—has reached the ear before you did.

Most stores don't appreciate this method of testing, but my last test for fresh corn involves popping one of the kernels with my fingernail. If the juice from the kernel is thick and milky, the corn is fresh. Be wary of markets that sell their produce out in the parking lot or a farmer who is selling corn in full sun. The sun will heat up the ears of corn and that will convert sugar to starch very quickly. I purchase from roadside stands and farmers who have their corn shaded from the sun.

One last item to check on your ear of corn is whether the area that has been broken off from the stalk has turned brown. Grandma always checked this area first because, she said, a brown stem meant the corn was at least two days old. For the freshest corn, look for ears whose stems have not darkened.

Storing

If you find yourself with extra corn or are unable to cook it the day you buy it, store it in your refrigerator with the husks left on. Do not store corn in a plastic bag. The cooling effect of the refrigerator will slow down the conversion from sugar to starch. If the stem is really long, shorten it to prevent loss of moisture. This will keep your corn fresh for a couple of days, but remember that the longer you store it, the less sugar and more starch you will have.

Because I live in Minnesota, fresh corn is only available during a short growing season. When I find a grower with fresh corn that is weighty and green, I purchase a couple dozen ears. I use some for lunch and supper, but I store a good deal of the corn for the winter. To do this, start by removing the husks and scrubbing the ear with a vegetable brush to remove the silk. Wash and drain the prepared cobs. Bring to a boil a large canning pot or kettle half filled with water. Prepare an ice bath to quickly cool the cobs. When the water begins to boil, blanch six ears at a time (to kill enzymes and stop the ripening process before freezing), allowing 7 minutes for small ears (1¼ inches or less in diameter), 9 minutes for medium, and 11 minutes for large (over 1½ inches in diameter). Remove from boiling water and put in ice bath to cool completely. This may take longer than the blanching. Drain cobs well and place in freezer bags, removing as much air as possible. I have a food vacuum, which makes this process so much easier. Write the date on your bags and place them in the freezer immediately. If using freezer bags, you can store them for up to eight months. If using a food vacuum, you can store them for up to three years. My corn on the cob has never lasted that long, because I cannot resist indulging through the first year.

MISCELLANEOUS

+ Do not add salt to water while soaking or boiling corn. It toughens the corn.
+ Overcooking hardens the kernels and reduces the sugar content.
+ Do not run cold water over cooked cobs to "cool them down" as it will make the corn soggy. Use an ice bath.

Corn and Roma Tomato Pasta Salad

1 pound penne pasta, cooked
1 tablespoon extra virgin olive oil
5 ears corn, cleaned and kernels cut off, or 5 cups frozen corn
8 medium roma tomatoes or two cups Canned Roma Tomatoes
    (see under The Basics), chopped
3 large garlic cloves, minced
3 cups spinach, washed and chopped
1 cup blue cheese, crumbled
Juice of freshly squeezed lemon
½ cup extra virgin olive oil
Kosher or Hawaiian salt
Freshly ground black pepper

1. Cook pasta per package instructions.
2. In a heavy-bottom skillet over medium heat, heat olive oil. Add corn and sauté, stirring occasionally, until sizzling and browning in spots.
3. In a large mixing bowl combine tomatoes, garlic, spinach, and cheese. Add cooked and drained pasta and sautéed corn. Toss and blend well. Sprinkle with lemon juice, olive oil, salt, and pepper. Toss again to blend and serve in large festive salad bowl. Set out a bowl with extra blue cheese crumbles for your guests to add later.

Serves six to eight.

Cherry Tomato Pie

I like to use a variety of heirloom cherry tomatoes such as Yellow Pear, Red Pear, Principe Borghese (an Italian heirloom variety), Green Grape, Red Cherry, and Gold Nugget. This mixture will create a colorful pie filling when cut and served.

Crust

3 cups all-purpose flour
1 tablespoon sugar
1 teaspoon kosher or Hawaiian salt
½ cup cold all-vegetable shortening, cut into small pieces
½ cup cold unsalted butter, cut into small pieces
½ cup cold water
1 large egg yolk and 1 teaspoon water for egg wash

"When the world wearies and society fails to satisfy, there is always the garden."

—Minnie Aumonier

1. All ingredients should be cold. Combine all the dry ingredients in a large mixing bowl. Add shortening and butter. Using a pastry blender, cut in the shortening and butter until the mixture resembles coarse meal.
2. Drop by drop, add the cold water. Mix in with the fingertips, not with the hands as the palms will warm the dough. Continue mixing water in until the dough begins to hold together without being sticky but not crumbly.
3. Divide dough into two pieces and place each in plastic wrap. Fold over plastic wrap and press down to form a disk. This will make rolling out easier after chilling. Finish wrapping in plastic and place in the refrigerator for at least 1 hour.
4. Lightly spray a 9-inch pie plate with butter or vegetable cooking spray. Roll out dough and place in pie plate. Return to the refrigerator until filling is ready. Roll out top crust.

Filling

2 tablespoons extra virgin olive oil
1 large onion, thinly sliced
1 large garlic clove, minced
2 tablespoons all-purpose flour
¼ teaspoon ground mustard
¼ teaspon freshly ground black pepper
1½ pounds assorted cherry tomatoes, sliced
1½ cups cheddar cheese, shredded
Kosher or Hawaiian salt

1. Preheat oven to 400 degrees. In a heavy-bottom skillet over medium, heat oil. Add onion and garlic. Cook until translucent. Do not brown the garlic as it will become bitter.
2. In a large mixing bowl, combine flour, mustard, and pepper. Blend in the cooked onions and cherry tomatoes. Stir to mix well.
3. Remove bottom pie crust from refrigerator and layer with half the cheese. Cover with tomato and onion mixture. Spread remaining cheese evenly over the mixture. Brush edges of pie crust with egg

wash. Attach top crust, fold edges together, and crimp. Create a decorative edge. Brush top crust with egg wash and sprinkle with kosher or Hawaiian salt.

4. Bake for 30 minutes. Remove from oven and let cool on a rack for 20 minutes before serving.

Serves six to eight.

⨍ Grilled Vegetables

1 pound fresh asparagus	Cherry tomatoes
1 fennel bulb	Beef steak tomatoes
1 large red onion	Extra virgin olive oil
1 large Vidalia onion	Kosher or Hawaiian salt
8–10 ounces portobello mushrooms	Freshly ground black pepper
8–10 ounces white button mushrooms	Fresh rosemary, chopped
	Fresh French or English thyme leaves
3 large bell peppers, red, green, yellow, or orange	Fresh French tarragon
1 sweet potato	Fresh chives
	Fresh sage leaves

1. Spray grill grate with cooking spray. Preheat to a medium heat. Wash vegetables and drain. Do not peel. Slice or cut into large chucks. Some vegetables may be easier to handle if you skewer them before grilling.
2. Brush with olive oil and season with salt and pepper.
3. Place on preheated grill but not directly over heat source. Grill all sides. Move to cooler part of grill as needed or to a warming rack. Five to 10 minutes before grilling is complete, sprinkle with fresh herbs. Place sage leaves on Vidalia onion slices, sprinkle sweet potato slices with chopped rosemary leaves, scatter chopped chives on portobello mushrooms, or sprinkle thyme leaves on tomatoes. Experiment and decide which you prefer. One of my favorite flavors for asparagus is to sprinkle freshly grated parmesan cheese immediately after removing from the grill.

⸕ Hobo Onions

I cannot make this recipe without thinking of my mother. This was one of her favorites, and she prepared it whenever sweet onions were available in Grand Forks. Vidalia onions were our favorite. I'm sure there was an origin for this recipe, but she never shared it. My folks liked the simple life and fancied themselves as "country folk." Mom always wanted to live in a log cabin in the woods. Her favorite vacation areas were the lakes near our home in Grand Forks such as those near Bemidji, Minnesota. Mom didn't want to go too far. I don't believe she ever suffered from wanderlust like I do. She was content with the Red River Valley. However, I wish I had been able to grant her wish of a log cabin in the woods where we could share Hobo Onions. I miss you, Mom.

Vidalia onions are mild and sweet enough to eat like fruit. The sugar content of this onion is comparable to that of an apple or a bottle of regular cola. Vidalia onions do not have the burn of average onions. If Vidalias are not available, other sweet onions, such as Walla Wallas, will do.

6 medium Vidalia or sweet onions, peeled and left whole
Extra virgin olive oil or unsalted butter or margarine (regular,
    low-fat, or fat-free)
Kosher or Hawaiian salt
Freshly ground black pepper
Fresh sage leaves

1. Preheat grill to a medium heat. Cut 6 (5-inch-square) sheets of foil, enough to envelop entire onion. Place onion in center of foil sheet. Drizzle with oil and sprinkle with salt and pepper. Bring corners up and fold around top of onion to hold in oil during cooking. Repeat for remaining onions.
2. Place foil-wrapped onions on grills but not directly over heat source. Cook for 30 to 40 minutes or until entire onion is tender and becoming translucent. Serve in foil pouch halfway unfolded with a sage leave on top.

Serves six.

ƒ Hobo Potatoes

My mother made these potatoes, as well as Hobo Onions, at every barbecue. No matter how large or how small the gathering, Mom would bring a baking sheet filled with a foil pouch for each guest. I've changed the recipe a bit, but it stills tastes fantastic. I have listed both ways to make this recipe. You can decide which you like better.

Mom's Version

> 3 pounds russet potatoes, cut into large chunks
> 2 packets dry onion soup mix
> ½ cup salted butter
> Salt and Pepper

1. In a mixing bowl combine potato chunks and dry onion soup mix. Cut 6 (5-inch-square) foil sheets. Spoon potato mixture onto center of foil sheet. Place 2 tablespoons butter on top of mixture. Season with salt and pepper. Bring corners of foil up to meet and create a foil pouch that closes on top. This will hold in melted butter while cooking.
2. Place on preheated grill but not directly over heat source. Cook for 40–45 minutes. Remove from heat and serve with extra butter, salt, and pepper.

Serves six.

"Let the farmer remember that every bird destroyed, and every nest robbed, is equivalent to a definite increase in insects with which he already has to struggle. He will soon appreciate the fact that he has a personal interest, and a strong one, in the preservation of birds."

—HENRY OLDYS

My Version

>   3 pounds russet potatoes, cut into large chunks
>   3 medium Vidalia or sweet onions, chopped
>   ⅓ cup extra virgin olive oil
>   Kosher or Hawaiian salt
>   Freshly ground black pepper

1. In a mixing bowl combine potato chunks, onions, and oil. Season with salt and pepper. Carefully spoon mixture into the center of a large (1-gallon) foil bag. Make sure there are no tears. Seal bag opening.
2. Place on preheated, medium heat grill but not directly over heat source. Cook for 45 minutes, turning once. Remove and serve.

Serves six.

Potato Fritters

This was my grandmother's version of steak fries. However you name them, they are always popular. These have replaced potato chips at every gathering we have, whether indoor or outdoor. Kosher or Hawaiian salt is a must for this recipe. You will not be disappointed.

>   3 pounds russet potatoes   Kosher or Hawaiian salt
>   ¼ cup extra virgin olive oil   Freshly ground black pepper

1. Preheat oven or grill to at least 400 degrees. Cut each potato in half. Place each half, cut side down, on cutting board and slice in half. Carefully hold together and slice each side of newly cut half to create lengthwise wedges.

"You know you are a gardener if you find compost a fascinating subject."

—AUTHOR UNKNOWN

2. Place sliced potatoes in a large mixing bowl. Drizzle with oil and sprinkle with a good deal of salt and pepper. Freshly ground cracked pepper makes this recipe absolutely come alive.

3. Place potato mixture in a 13- × 9-inch baking pan (for the grill) or a large jelly roll pan (for the oven) sprayed with cooking spray. Cook for 50 to 60 minutes, depending on temperature. Shake pan or re-distribute with spatula every 20 minutes. Remove from oven. Place in plastic cups or glasses lined with napkins or paper towels. Sprinkle with additional salt and serve with malt vinegar, mayonnaise (regular, low-fat, or fat-free), and tomato catsup.

Serves six to eight.

Cornbread with Honey

4 cups all-purpose flour, unsifted
1½ cups yellow cornmeal
1 teaspoon kosher or Hawaiian salt
1½ tablespoons baking powder
1 tablespoon sugar
2 tablespoons unsalted butter, melted
3 large eggs
1 cup milk (regular, low-fat, or vanilla soy)
1¼ cups corn kernels, freshly cut from the cob or frozen
Honey for drizzling, preferably honey from the island of Kauai

1. Preheat oven to 400 degrees. Spray an 8-inch-square cake pan or 8-inch iron skillet with cooking spray. Set aside.

2. In a large mixing bowl combine, flour, cornmeal, salt, and baking powder. Stir in sugar and create a well in the center of the dry ingredients. Pour melted butter, eggs, and milk into well. Beat until dry ingredients are just moistened.

3. With spatula or back of a wooden spoon, fold corn kernels into corn-bread mixture.

4. Pour into prepared pan or skillet. Bake for 20–25 minutes or until a cake tester inserted into the center comes out clean. Remove from oven and cool on a rack for 10 minutes. Invert pan and release cornbread onto a serving plate. Cut into wedges and serve warm. Pour honey into a decorative glass or honey pot for serving.

Serves eight.

Kabobs

1. Choose Your Meats and Vegetables

- Beef—cut into 1½-inch cubes
- Ground beef or pork—made into 1½-inch meatballs, filled if desired (see step 4)
- Pork—cut into 1¼-inch cubes
- Poultry—cut into 1-inch chunks
- Sausage—cut into ¾-inch rounds
- Shrimp—peeled and deveined
- Scallops—ready as is
- Vegetables—cubed or sliced
- Fruit—cubed or sliced

2. Marinate (see marinade recipes later in this chapter)

- Beef—Beer, Red Wine, Teriyaki, or Onion Marinade
- Pork—Pineapple or Teriyaki Marinade
- Poultry—Apple Cider or Teriyaki Marinade
- Seafood—White Wine or Teriyaki Marinade

3. Parboil

- Corn on the cob (cut into bite-sized chunks), small white onions, carrots, or other root vegetables. Partially cook by boiling so that grilling times will be the same as for the other foods.

4. Prepare

- Soak—If using wooden skewers soak 1 hour in water to prevent burning.
- Fill—Stuff meatballs with mushrooms, olives, blue cheese, pineapple, or water chestnuts. Pierce with skewer to secure both meat and stuffing.
- Construct—Assemble food on skewer and marinate until ready to cook.

5. Grill (at medium temperature)

- Beef—15 minutes, turning frequently
- Ground beef—20 minutes, turning frequently
- Pork—18 minutes, turning frequently
- Poultry—20 minutes, turning frequently
- Sausage—15 minutes, turning frequently
- Shrimp—5 minutes, turning frequently
- Scallops—5 minutes, turning frequently
- Vegetables—15 to 20 minutes, turning frequently
- Fruit—5 to 10 minutes, turning frequently

6. Sauces to Brush On (grilling at medium temperature)

- Beef—Barbecue, teriyaki, Worcestershire sauce, prepared mustard, or soy sauce
- Ground beef—Barbecue, teriyaki, prepared mustard, or soy sauce
- Pork—Barbecue, teriyaki, Worcestershire sauce, soy sauce, honey, or pineapple juice
- Poultry—Barbecue, teriyaki, prepared mustard, or soy sauce
- Sausage—Beer, barbecue, teriyaki, prepared mustard, or soy sauce
- Shrimp—Olive oil, unsalted butter, or lemon juice
- Scallops—Olive oil, unsalted butter, or lemon juice
- Vegetables—Olive oil or unsalted butter mixed with fresh herbs
- Fruit—unsalted butter, brown sugar, cinnamon, nutmeg, and lemon juice mixed together

Marinades

Heat all marinades in a heavy-bottom saucepan until sugars dissolve and flavors begin to meld. Do not let marinade boil. Remove it from heat and cool completely before using. Place meats, seafoods, or vegetables in a container with a cover that can be secured tightly. I use zipper storage bags or my food vacuum. The food vacuum also reduces marinating time by removing the air from the bag. It's amazing. Let all kabob items marinate at least 4 hours or overnight.

Apple Cider

1 cup apple cider
¼ cup white vinegar
½ cup green onions, chopped with greens
¼ cup extra virgin olive oil
1 teaspoon kosher or Hawaiian salt
½ teaspoon freshly ground black pepper

Beer

1 12-ounce can of beer
½ cup extra virgin olive oil
¼ cup cider vinegar
½ cup green onions, chopped with greens
2 large garlic cloves, minced
1 teaspoon kosher or Hawaiian salt
½ teaspoon freshly ground black pepper

Onion

1 large onion, chopped
1 large garlic clove, minced
½ cup extra virgin olive oil
¼ cup cider vinegar
1½ teaspoons baker's superfine sugar
2 teaspoons Worcestershire sauce

Pineapple

  1 cup fresh pineapple, peeled and pureed in a blender
  1 large garlic clove, minced
  ½ cup sherry cooking wine
  3 tablespoons dark brown sugar

Red Wine

  1 cup good-quality red wine
  ½ cup extra virgin olive oil
  ½ cup sweet onion, chopped
  2 large garlic cloves, minced
  1 teaspoon kosher or Hawaiian salt
  ½ teaspoon freshly ground black pepper

Teriyaki

  1 cup soy sauce
  1 large garlic clove, minced
  ½ cup sherry cooking wine
  ½ cup dark brown sugar
  ¼ cup white vinegar
  ¼ cup extra virgin olive oil

White Wine

  1 cup good-quality white wine
  ¾ cup freshly squeezed lemon or lime juice
  ½ teaspoon ground mustard
  1 teaspoon kosher or Hawaiian salt
  ½ teaspoon freshly ground black pepper

✟ Pulled Pork

The success of this recipe is in the slow cooking. You will reward your guests with tender, moist meat, rich in savory flavors. I prefer to slow-cook in my barbecue grill, but you may use an oven. Using a barbecue or covered grill adds a smoky essence that you cannot achieve with a conventional oven. When I do prepare the meat in my oven, I add 1 tablespoon liquid smoke to my barbecue sauce.

7 pounds pork, picnic, butt roast, or shoulder

Pork Rub (1 tablespoon of each ingredient)

Freshly ground black pepper	Kosher or Hawaiian salt
Dark brown sugar	Ground mustard
Paprika	Onion powder
Cayenne pepper	

1. In a plastic bag or mixing bowl, combine black pepper, sugar, paprika, cayenne, salt, mustard, and onion powder.
2. Rub pork on all sides with half of the rub mixture. Place in a 1-gallon or larger plastic bag and close tightly. Refrigerate overnight. Remove next morning and pat with half of the remaining rub mixture. Save some for the barbecue sauce. Let rubbed pork rest 1 hour at room temperature.

Barbecue Sauce

3 cups cider vinegar	4 tablespoons freshly ground black pepper
4 large garlic cloves, minced	
1 large onion, finely chopped	1 teaspoon cayenne pepper
1 cup water	2 tablespoons kosher or Hawaiian salt
1 tablespoon ground mustard	

1. Preheat barbecue grill or oven to about 250 degrees. Do not heat above 275 degrees.
2. In a heavy-bottom saucepan, combine vinegar, garlic, onion, water, mustard, black and cayenne peppers, and salt. Add any remaining rub to barbecue sauce mixture. Simmer over low heat for half an hour, stirring frequently to prevent boiling.
3. Place rubbed pork in a foil pan or roaster and seal tightly with foil so that moisture won't escape. Apply barbecue sauce to meat every 45 minutes. Let the pork steam in its own juice for around 4 to 5 hours. Internal temperature needs to be between 170 to 180 degrees on a meat thermometer.
4. When cooked meat is fork tender, pull from bone, shred, and moisten with sauce. Serve with remaining barbecue sauce on buns or bread rolls.

Serves ten to twelve.

⨍ Blue Cheese–Stuffed Hamburgers

Find a good-quality aged blue cheese like Maytag Blue Cheese from Iowa. Check out a local market that specializes in quality cheeses and chat about what makes each cheese unique. The staff will be happy to answer any of your questions and offer you samples.

2 pounds lean ground beef
½ teaspoon freshly ground
    black pepper
½ teaspoon kosher or
    Hawaiian salt
1 large onion, diced
2 tablespoons
    Worcestershire sauce
1 cup blue cheese, crumbled

4 ounces cream cheese
    (regular, low-fat, or fat-free),
    room temperature
1 tablespoon Dijon mustard
Lettuce
Onion, thinly sliced
Beefsteak tomatoes
6 buns or bread rolls

1. Preheat barbecue grill to medium. In a mixing bowl, combine ground beef, pepper, salt, onions, and Worcestershire sauce. Form 12 patties about ¼ inch thick. Set aside.
2. In a medium mixing bowl, beat cream cheese with an electric mixer until fluffy. Stir in blue cheese and mustard.
3. Spoon 2 tablespoons of the cheese mixture on the middle of 6 meat patties. Place remaining meat patties on top and press edges together to seal in cheese mixture.
4. Place hamburgers on grill about 15 minutes per side. Turn once.
5. Remove from barbecue grill and place on buns. Top with lettuce, onions, and tomatoes.

Serves six.

Summer Stew (Barbecue Stew)

Grandma called this stew something different every time she prepared it. She had it listed in her recipe books as Summer Stew or Barbecue Stew. It's very much like Low Country Shrimp Boil or Frogmore Stew found in other recipe books. Regardless of the name, it tastes fantastic and deserves a hearty biscuit as accompaniment. Grandma would boil this stew on the grill, drain it, and pour it out on top of several layers of newspapers instead of serving in bowls or on plates. She would then bring out a basket of her ham biscuits and a pitcher of apricot nectar. It was heaven. I have difficulty finding apricot nectar, so I bring out a couple of large cans of Australian beer to make up for the loss.

    5 quarts water
    ½ cup shrimp and crab boil spices
    6 medium red potatoes
    7 ears corn, shucked and cut in thirds
    1 large onion, cut in quarters
    ½ pound smoked sausage, cut into chunks
    2 pounds shrimp, cleaned and deveined, with tails on
    Lemon wedges
    Cocktail sauce

1. In an 8-quart stockpot, large kettle, or cast iron bean pot, bring water to a boil over a grill fire or stove top. Add boil spices and potatoes. Cook until fork tender. Remove potatoes from water and set aside in a covered bowl.
2. Add corn, onion, and sausage. Bring water back to a hard boil. Cook for 10 minutes. Add shrimp and cooked potatoes. Cook for 5 minutes or until shrimp turns pink and begin to float. Do not overcook shrimp, as they will become tough or mushy.
3. Remove from heat and drain. Serve on a large platter or pour drained contents onto several layers of newspaper covering the table in front of your guests. If you serve up the old-fashioned way, make sure you put out a roll of paper towels. Serve with lemon wedges, your favorite cocktail sauce, and Grandma's Ham Biscuits (see next recipe).

Serves six.

⸏ Grandma's Ham Biscuits

Unlike the more common wet-cured ham, which is soaked in brine or injected with a salt solution, country ham is dry-cured and aged for a much longer period. Wet-cured hams have a lot of water, so they have a watery flavor. The flavor of country hams is more concentrated. Government guidelines require that at least 18 percent of the ham's original weight be lost during the curing and aging process. Longer aging takes that figure over 20 percent. In most cases, the aging is just under one year. Today, most local markets sell ready-to-eat whole country hams and even just slices. There is one obstacle, however—salt. By law, the salt content of country hams must be at least 4 percent. However, the salty taste is what makes country hams so unique. By using country ham as an ingredient in other dishes, such as Grandma's Ham Biscuits, rather than as the centerpiece of the meal, you can avoid a meal high in salt.

"There is no such thing as an ugly garden. Gardens, like babies, are all beautiful to their parents."

—Ken Druse

---

2 cups all-purpose flour
2 teaspoons baking powder
½ teaspoon kosher or Hawaiian salt
4 tablespoons lard or all-vegetable shortening
⅔ cup milk
⅔ cup country ham, minced
½ teaspoon yellow mustard
2 tablespoons unsalted butter, melted
Milk for brushing

1. Preheat oven to 450 degrees. Spray a baking pan with cooking spray. In a large mixing bowl, combine flour, baking powder, and salt. Using a pastry blender, cut in lard or shortening. Slowly add milk and stir with a fork until dough starts to form.
2. On a lightly floured surface, pour out dough. Knead until well blended and a soft dough is formed. Roll out dough until about ½ inch thick.
3. Cut out 24 biscuit rounds using a floured 1½-inch biscuit cutter. Place rounds on baking pan and brush with melted butter.
4. In a small bowl stir together ham and mustard. Add about ½ teaspoon of ham mixture on top of biscuit rounds. Top with remaining biscuit rounds. Brush with remaining milk.
5. Bake for 10-15 minutes or until golden. Serve warm with extra butter or margarine.

Makes twenty-four.

Lemon-Dill Salmon Steaks

When purchasing salmon steak, make sure to find the freshest salmon possible. Find a steak that is tight with no gaps. Also, the salmon steaks should not have a strong "fishy" smell; the odor should be mild. Purchase salmon steaks with the skin intact. The skin will prevent the salmon from curling up or flaking while on the barbecue grill. I serve my salmon with the skin on as it will easily peel off after cooking. Keep salmon refrigerated or on ice until it is ready to be grilled.

4 medium salmon steaks with skin on
½ cup freshly squeezed lemon juice
3 tablespoons extra virgin olive oil
1 tablespoon fresh dill, minced
½ teaspoon kosher or Hawaiian salt
½ teaspoon white pepper
Lemon wedges

1. In a container with a cover or a large plastic bag, combine lemon juice, oil, dill, salt, and pepper. Place salmon in container and coat with marinade on all sides. Cover or seal tightly. Refrigerate for at least 4 hours or overnight.
2. Preheat barbecue grill to a medium heat. Place salmon steaks, skin side down, about 4 inches from heat source but not directly over. Close barbecue lid and grill for about 5 minutes. Turn only once.
3. Salmon will continue to cook after it has been removed from the grill. Cook just until the meat begins to change color and becomes flaky. Insert a knife near the bone or the thickest part of the salmon steak. Well-done salmon will flake effortlessly. Serve with lemon wedges and Dill Sauce (see under The Basics).

Serves four.

Grilled Pineapple

This recipe is similar to grilling vegetables except that the pineapple provides its own grilling sauce, which caramelizes as it cooks. I used to sauté pineapple wedges in a heavy-bottom skillet with melted butter and a sprinkle of sugar. However, when we lived on the island of Kauai for one week, we grilled almost every meal, so I sliced the pineapple into wedges and simply placed them on the grill away from the direct heat. I didn't need the melted butter or sprinkling of sugar. The pineapple did just fine on its own.

We were fortunate to be able to purchase freshly picked pineapple from a beautiful exotic vegetable and fruit stand near Poipu Beach where our rental house was located. One day while I was visiting the stand for goodies, the owner explained that the pineapple develops from many small fruits fused together. It is both juicy and fleshy, with the stem serving as the fibrous core. The tough, waxy rind may be dark green, yellow, orangish-yellow, or reddish when the fruit is ripe. But the best fruit on the island of Kauai is orangish yellow at the bottom and hard to the touch. It should also emit a sweet pineapple fragrance from the bottom of the fruit.

1 large freshly picked pineapple

1. Preheat barbecue grill to a medium heat. With a sharp knife, carefully slice the top off the pineapple. Cut the pineapple down the middle and remove about half inch of the core. With the fruit side down, slice each half into six wedges leaving the rough rind attached.
2. Place pineapple wedges, fruit side down, on grill grate away from direct heat source. Turn often to grill both sides of each wedge. Fruit will begin to brown and have grate marks when cooked.
3. Remove from heat and serve plain or with ice cream.

Serves six with two wedges each.

"An optimistic gardener is one who believes that whatever goes down must come up."

—LESLIE HALL

⨍ Exotic Fruits Skewers

This recipe was also inspired by the island of Kauai and the wonderful exotic fruits that were available daily. Once I returned home, I searched for exotic fruits to serve at any gathering. It delights my guests to try fruits they have never heard of or tasted.

1 mango, peeled, pitted, and cut into chunks
1 papaya, peeled, seeded, and cut into chunks
2 bananas, cut into thick slices
2 star fruit, cut into thick slices
3 kiwi, peeled and cut into thick slices
12 lemon leaves
½ cup sugar
½ cup pure maple syrup
8 ounces cream cheese (low-fat or fat-free), room temperature
8 ounces fat-free half-and-half
1 lime, freshly squeezed and grated for zest
3 tablespoons confectioner's sugar

1. Preheat grill to medium. Soak 6 wooden skewers in water for 30 minutes. Layer a baking pan with foil folded up around the edges. Spray with cooking spray. Set aside.
2. Assemble each skewer with two pieces of each fruit in rotation and lemon leaves—two leaves per skewer. Set finished skewer on prepared foil.
3. In small bowl mix sugar and maple syrup. Brush over fruit skewers. Place baking pan on grill and cover. Cook for 5 to 10 minutes until fruit begins to release its sugars and mangos turn golden.
4. In a mixing bowl, beat cream cheese with an electric mixer until fluffy. Beat in half-and-half, lime juice, zest, and confectioner's sugar.
6. Remove skewers from grill. Brush cream cheese mixture over skewers and serve immediately.

Serves six.

⸖ Champagne Raspberry Parfait

Champagne is mother's milk to me. I have adored this drink since I was legally able to consume it. (Well, actually, before then also.)

Serve in a variety of glasses to create a mood and add to the conversation. I've offered this adult dessert to my guests in pilsner glasses, martini glasses, high balls, and parfait glasses. I'm sure there are other wonderful ways to serve it, but that is for you to decide. Use blackberries, baby strawberries, cherries, or blueberries. I've even used golden berries (also known as ground cherries) and currants.

2 envelopes unflavored gelatin
1 cup water
¾ cup superfine baker's sugar
1 750-ml bottle champagne
2 pints fresh raspberries
2 tablespoons superfine baker's sugar

1. In a heavy-bottom saucepan, combine gelatin and water. Let soften for 5 minutes. Turn heat to low and stir gently until gelatin dissolves. Do not let boil. Add sugar and blend. Remove from heat. Continue stirring mixture until sugar has completely dissolved. Pour in champagne and blend well.
2. Pour champagne mixture into a baking pan and cover. Refrigerate overnight or until set, which can take up to 12 hours.
3. Set parfait, pilsner, or large martini glasses on a serving tray. Toss raspberries with baker's sugar. Spoon champagne gelatin chunks into glasses. Layer gelatin and raspberries until all ingredients are used. End with a top layer of raspberries. Chill until ready to serve.

Serves eight.

⸙ Lemon-Lime Cheesecake

I love any citrus dessert at a barbecue gathering. This cheesecake requires no baking and may be prepared a day ahead of time. Award your guests with this luxury and savor the raves you'll garner. There is no need to tell anyone that you didn't have to sweat over a hot oven to complete this fabulous dessert.

> 1½ cups graham crackers (regular or reduced fat), finely ground
> 1 cup sugar, divided
> ¼ cup unsalted butter, melted
> 2 lemons, freshly squeezed and grated for zest
> 1 envelope unflavored gelatin
> 1 cup whole-milk ricotta cheese, preferably ewe's milk ricotta
> ⅔ cup heavy whipping cream
> 2 large eggs, separated
> 3 limes, freshly squeezed and grated for zest
> 1 teaspoon arrowroot
> 2 tablespoons water

1. Spray a 9-inch springform pan with cooking spray. Set aside. In the bowl of a food processor, combine graham crackers and ⅓ cup sugar. Process to a fine crumb. Add melted butter and process until butter has been incorporated into crumb mixture. Press ground mixture into bottom of springform pan. Place in freezer until cheesecake filling is ready.

2. In a heavy-bottom saucepan, stir together lemon juice, zest, and gelatin. Let soften for 5 minutes. Turn heat to low and stir gently until the gelatin has dissolved. Remove from heat and cool.

3. In a mixing bowl, beat together the ricotta cheese and ⅓ cup sugar. Blend in the heavy cream and egg yolks. Add cooled gelatin mixture and whisk together well.

4. Beat egg whites with an electric mixer until they form soft peaks. Gently fold in cheese mixture. Pour over chilled crust. Refrigerate for at least 4 hours.

5. In a heavy bottom saucepan, add lime juice, zest, and ⅓ cup sugar. Bring to a boil. Stirring constantly, boil for 5 minutes. Mix arrowroot with 2 tablespoons water. Blend arrowroot mixture with syrup and return to a boil. Boil for 2 minutes or until mixture begins to thicken. Cool to room temperature and store in refrigerator.

6. Carefully remove cheesecake from springform pan. Place on a decorative cake plate and spoon chilled lime syrup over cheesecake.

Serves twelve to sixteen.

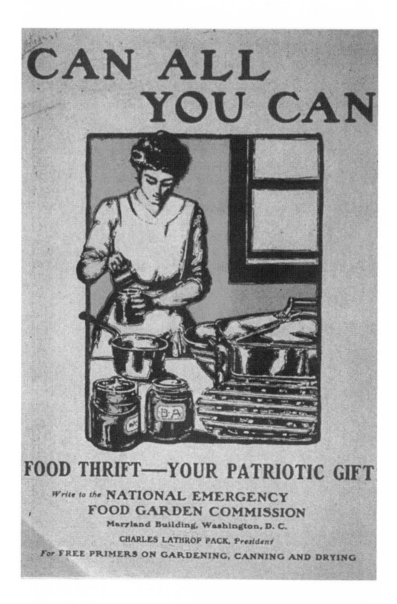

Festival of the Moonflower

*T*HIS GATHERING BEGAN some years ago during a visit to my best friend's home. I had been growing moonflowers (*Ipomoea alba*) for many years. My best friend, Dan Kenward, and his partner, Ron Iverson, decided to plant moonflower seeds on their deck in a large container. When we arrived, they served cocktails on the deck, and I commented on the flowers. They complained that their moonflowers had yet to bloom. I looked at the trailing vines and pointed to a large unfurling bud, exclaiming that they had a flower that was going to open that evening. Hence began the Festival of the Moonflower.

Moonflowers open in the evenings toward the end of August so that they can be pollinated by night-flying moths. Isn't that remarkable? Like most moth-pollinated flowers, the moonflower is white, which attracts the moths. This fantastic flower is a close relative of my all-time favorite flower, the morning glory (*Ipomoea purpurea*), which opens in the morning so that it can be pollinated by bees and other insects that are active during the day. Sadly, moonflower petals die the morning after they open. Here in the Twin Cities of Minnesota, the moonflower begins to open its buds around 6:00 p.m., so plan to have your guests arrive and have cocktails in hand before the impressive opening.

I adore entertaining my guests, or just my partner and myself, on our patio in the evening. With twinkle lights in the arbors, torches along the garden paths, and candles scattered around the yard, night becomes a time to craft astonishing moods. The radio is always turned to a local station that plays big band, swing, and old radio shows featuring George Burns and Gracie Allen or Jack Benny. The garden seems to get pleasure from this station, and so do I. However, some evenings the only music we need is the insect's song.

Growing flowers that open at night is extraordinary and exciting. Luckily, there are many plants that work the night shift. Some have flowers that open only at night to radiate their wonderful fragrance. This is an astonishing strategy because it is meant to attract night-pollinating moths. Some have flowers that are more fragrant at night, and others just look better at night because of their white, glowing flowers or silvery leaves. Gardens designed around white flowers and silver-leaved plants are striking both day and night, however, so they will delight your guests at any time. The vines of the moonflower and morning glory move slowly and dramatically toward and away from a light source in an almost serpent-like tango during the night. I've watched for hours in astonishment as they weave as if they were underwater when they are near the twinkle lights in an arbor. They will mesmerize your guests (or make them believe the cocktails are a bit too strong!).

The moonflower is my show stopper, and we have designed a gathering around its opening night. The spiraled flower buds flirt with you during the day as you anticipate the show. The six-inch-wide white flowers start opening around dusk. I invite everyone to get up close to inhale the flower's passionate fragrance. Grow the vine so that it scrambles over arbors and onto large trellises. I have grown both morning glory and moonflower together on arbors or trellises to allow for both morning and evening flowering. They complement each other beautifully.

Other night fragrant flowers include night-blooming jasmine, flowering tobacco, and sweet autumn clematis. Silvery leaved plants such as lamb's ear and artemesias reflect the moonlight. Don't stop enjoying your garden just because the sun has set.

You may not appreciate moonflowers as much as I do, but this chapter invites you to create a gathering around something that thrills you and that you enjoy sharing with your friends and family, extended or otherwise.

SUGGESTED SELECTIONS FOR YOUR
FESTIVAL OF THE MOONFLOWER

- Frozen Whiskey Sours
- Frozen Midori Sours
- Relish Tray
  - Grandma's Sweet Cucumber Relish
  - Corn Relish
  - Flamboyant Pepper Relish
  - Zucchini Relish
  - Vidalia Onion Relish
  - Crispy Thin Homemade Crackers
- Vegetable Medley Pizza
- Bacon Cheeseburger Pizza
- Dill Pickle Dip

All these selections may be served on a patio table with candles. I use an antique candleholder that looks like a prop from *The Phantom of the Opera,* or you could use something more modern that holds five or more candles. Moonflowers, great food, cocktails, and the night-flying moths will transport you and your guests to a place right out of *Dr. Doolittle.*

⸙ Frozen Whiskey Sours

1 cup orange juice, divided

1 cup good-quality whiskey
   or bourbon

½ cup Sour Mix (see under The Basics)

4 cups ice

Vanilla sugar

Mint leaves

1. Pour about ¼ cup orange juice into a small bowl or plate with a raised rim. In another bowl or plate, sprinkle a layer of vanilla sugar. Dip rim of tumbler or rock glass, until well coated, in orange juice and press into vanilla sugar to coat. Place glasses in freezer until ready to serve.
2. In a blender add remaining orange juice, whiskey, sour mix, and ice. Pulse until mixture resembles slush.
3. Pour blended cocktail mixture into chilled glasses. Garnish with a half slice of orange and a sprig of mint leaves.

Serves four.

⸙ Frozen Midori Sours

2 cups Sour Mix
   (see under The Basics)

1 cup Midori

4 cups ice

Mint leaves

Guava juice for the rim of the glass

Vanilla sugar

1. Pour about ¼ cup guava juice into a small bowl or plate with a raised rim. In another bowl or plate, sprinkle a layer of vanilla sugar. Dip rim of tumbler or rock glass, until well coated, in guava juice and press into vanilla sugar to coat. Place glasses in freezer until ready to serve.
2. In a blender add sour mix, Midori, and ice. Pulse until mixture resembles slush.
3. Pour blended cocktail mixture into chilled glasses. Garnish with mint leaves.

Serves four.

✗ Relish Tray

I know you can find jars of relish at your local grocer, but I challenge you to find a better-tasting old-fashioned relish than my grandma's Sweet Cucumber Relish. This recipe has taken First Place Cucumber Relish 2002 at the Minnesota State Fair, Best Overall Relish of the 2002 Minnesota State Fair awarded by Gedney Pickle Company, and Third Place Cucumber Relish in both 2003 and 2004, also at the Minnesota State Fair. Nor will you find a more remarkable "out of the ordinary" relish than my Vidalia Onion Relish, which took First Place Relish for 2001, 2002, and 2003, also at the Minnesota State Fair. (Since I have won first place three years running, Minnesota State Fair rules state that I must "sit out" for the next two years. I think that allows me bragging rights.) I order my Vidalia onions early each spring from a farm in Georgia. In the middle of May, my fifty pounds of Vidalia onions arrive, and I get busy putting up several dozen jars for myself, friends, and next year's holiday gifts. I offer these recipes to you as a wonderful treat to serve to your guests.

I suggest that you put each relish in matching decorative bowls and place around a plate with softened cream cheese (regular, low-fat, or fat-free). Invite your guests to spread a little softened cream cheese on a cracker, then add a spoonful of relish and enjoy! It's a delicious treat and, if you are using fat-free cream cheese and reduced fat crackers, an almost fat-free delight as relish has no fat. I've also sprinkled dried herbs such as basil or oregano on top of the softened cream cheese to add a bit of zest. Also, make sure that your pickling salt, celery seed, mustard seed, and powdered turmeric are fresh. I would suggest no older than six months.

Important: Before attempting to can or preserve, please read carefully all USDA safety instructions. You may view the *USDA Complete Guide to Home Canning* at http://edis.ifas.ufl.edu/TOPIC_Canning_Food or http://foodsafety.cas.psu.edu/canningguide.html.

⸎ Grandma's Sweet Cucumber Relish

2002 Winner, Best Overall Relish, Minnesota State Fair awarded by Gedney Pickle Company; 2002 Winner, First Place Cucumber Relish, Minnesota State Fair; 2003 and 2004 Winner, Third Place Cucumber Relish, Minnesota State Fair

6 medium cucumbers	3 cups sugar
3 sweet red peppers	2 cups cider vinegar
6 medium Vidalia or	2½ teaspoons celery seed
sweet onions	2½ teaspoons mustard seed
½ cup pickling salt	½ teaspoon powdered turmeric

1. Choose medium cucumbers with few or no seeds. Wash the cucumbers and peppers. Discard stems and seeds from the peppers. Using a food processor, chop cucumbers and peppers separately into small bits (chopped cucumbers should produce no liquid; that is the true measure of a successfully crisp and chunky relish). Measure 6 cups cucumbers and 3 cups peppers. Peel onions and chop in processor; measure 6 cups. Combine cucumbers, peppers, and onions in a large crock, stainless steel, glass, or unchipped enamel bowl. Sprinkle with pickling salt; add ice cold water to cover. Let stand, covered, at room temperature for 2 hours.

2. Pour mixture into a colander and drain well in the sink. Rinse with fresh cool water and drain again. While the mixture is draining, in a large kettle or 8-quart Dutch oven combine sugar, vinegar, celery seed, mustard seed, and turmeric. Heat to boiling on medium heat. Add drained vegetable mixture, turn heat to medium-high, and return to boiling. Cook uncovered and stir to make sure relish does not burn. Continue to cook for about 10 minutes until any excess liquid has evaporated.

3. Thoroughly wash and scald 8 half-pint jars. Keep hot until needed. Prepare lids according to manufacturer's directions.

4. Remove cooked relish from heat. Immediately ladle into hot jars, leaving ¼-inch headspace. Remove air bubbles by running a plastic knife around the inside edge of the jar. Wipe jar rims; seal with hot

lids and screw bands. Process filled jars in a boiling-water canner for 10 minutes. Remove jars from canner and cool on racks.

Makes eight half-pints.

Corn Relish

2002, 2003, and 2004 Winner, Third Place Corn Relish, Minnesota State Fair

> 8 cups fresh or frozen corn (approximately 1 dozen ears)
> 2 cups water
> 3 cups celery, chopped (approximately 6 stalks)
> 1½ cups red bell pepper, chopped
> 1½ cups green bell pepper, chopped
> 1 cup Vidalia or sweet onion, chopped
> 2½ cups white vinegar
> 1¾ cups sugar
> 4 teaspoons dry mustard
> 2 teaspoons pickling salt
> 2 teaspoons celery seed
> 1 teaspoon powdered turmeric
> 3 tablespoons cornstarch
> 2 tablespoons water

1. In a large kettle or 8-quart Dutch oven combine corn and water. Bring to a boil and reduce heat to low. Simmer, covered, about 5 minutes or until the corn is nearly tender. Drain in a colander.
2. Using the same kettle or Dutch oven, combine corn, celery, red and green bell peppers, and onion. Blend in vinegar, sugar, mustard, pickling salt, celery seed, and turmeric. Bring mixture to a boil. Boil, with bubbles slowly rising to the top of the relish mixture, for 5 minutes, stirring occasionally. In a small bowl, combine cornstarch and water. Add to corn relish mixture. Relish will become thick and bubbly. Continue cooking for 1 minute.

3. Thoroughly wash and scald 8 half-pint jars. Keep hot until needed. Prepare lids according to manufacturer's directions.

4. Remove cooked relish from heat. Immediately ladle into hot jars, leaving ½-inch headspace. Remove air bubbles by running a plastic knife around the inside edge of the jar. Add more relish to maintain the headspace, if necessary. Wipe jar rims; seal with hot lids and screw bands. Process filled jars in a boiling-water canner for 20 minutes. Remove jars from canner and cool on racks.

Makes eight half-pints.

Flamboyant Pepper Relish

2002 and 2004 Winner, Third Place Pepper Relish,
Minnesota State Fair

4 red bell peppers	2 medium Vidalia or sweet onions,
2 green bell peppers	finely chopped
2 yellow bell peppers	2 cups cider vinegar
2 orange bell peppers	1¼ cups sugar
2 purple bell peppers	1 tablespoon pickling salt

1. Rinse and drain the bell peppers. Remove the seeds and membranes. Chop into little pieces that resemble small jewels. You may also chop in a food processor, but be careful not to process to a mushy pulp.

2. In a large crock, stainless steel, glass, or unchipped enamel bowl, combine the peppers and onions. Add boiling water to cover the vegetables. Let stand for 10 minutes. Drain in a colander and return to crock or bowl. Cover again with boiling water. Let stand for 5 minutes. Drain again. Allow the peppers and onions to drain in the colander for at least 1 hour.

3. While the mixture is draining, in a large kettle or 8-quart Dutch oven combine vinegar, sugar, and salt. Bring to a boil. Add drained vegetable mixture, turn heat to medium, and simmer for 15 minutes. Cook uncovered and stir frequently to prevent relish sticking or scorching.

4. Thoroughly wash and scald 8 half-pint jars. Keep hot until needed. Prepare lids according to manufacturer's directions.

5. Remove cooked relish from heat. Immediately ladle into hot jars, leaving ½-inch headspace. Remove air bubbles by running a plastic knife around the inside edge of the jar. Add more relish to maintain the headspace, if necessary. Wipe jar rims; seal with hot lids and screw bands. Process filled jars in a boiling-water canner for 15 minutes. Remove jars from canner and cool on racks.

Makes eight half-pints.

Zucchini Relish

2004 Winner, Second Place Zucchini Relish, Minnesota State Fair

> 2 cups medium-sized zucchini, finely chopped
> 2 medium Vidalia or sweet onions, finely chopped
> 2 green bell peppers, finely chopped
> ¼ cup canning salt
> 2¼ cups sugar
> 2¼ cups white vinegar
> ½ teaspoon ground cloves
> 1 teaspoon powdered turmeric
> 1 teaspoon dry mustard
> 1 teaspoon celery seed
> 1 teaspoon mustard seed

1. Chop zucchini and onions. Rinse and drain the bell peppers. Remove the seeds and membranes. Chop into little pieces that resemble small jewels. You may also chop in a food processor, but be careful not to process to a mushy pulp. Using a food processor will give your relish vegetables a uniform shape.

2. In a large crock, stainless steel, glass, or unchipped enamel bowl, combine all the vegetables. Mix salt with just enough water to dissolve. Add to vegetables. Using cold water, cover vegetable mixture

and let stand in a cool place at least 3 hours. Drain in a colander. Rinse with cold water and drain again. Gently press the vegetables to extract as much water as possible.

3. While the mixture is draining, in a large kettle or 8-quart Dutch oven combine sugar, vinegar, cloves, turmeric, dry mustard, celery seeds, and mustard seeds. Add drained vegetable mixture and blend well. Bring to a boil over medium-high heat. Gently boil for 5 minutes, stirring frequently to prevent relish sticking or scorching.

4. Thoroughly wash and scald 8 half-pint jars. Keep hot until needed. Prepare lids according to manufacturer's directions.

5. Remove cooked relish from heat. Immediately ladle into hot jars, leaving ½-inch headspace. Remove air bubbles by running a plastic knife around the inside edge of the jar. Add more relish to maintain the headspace, if necessary. Wipe jar rims; seal with hot lids and screw bands. Process filled jars in a boiling-water canner for 10 minutes. Remove jars from canner and cool on racks.

Makes eight half-pints.

Vidalia Onion Relish

2001, 2002, and 2003 Winner, First Place Relish
Not Otherwise Specified, Minnesota State Fair

    10 cups finely chopped Vidalia onions (about 5 to 10 medium to
       large onions)
    2 large red bell peppers, chopped
    ½ cup canning salt
    3 cups cider vinegar
    3 cups sugar
    2 teaspoons mustard seed
    2 teaspoons celery seed
    1 teaspoon powdered turmeric

1. Place chopped onions, peppers, and salt in a large crock, stainless steel, glass, or unchipped enamel bowl. Cover with ice water and let stand 1 hour. Drain in a colander, rinse with cold water, and drain again.
2. In a large kettle or 8-quart Dutch oven, mix vinegar, sugar, mustard seed, celery seed, and turmeric. Bring to a boil over medium-high heat, stirring to dissolve sugar. Add onions and peppers; boil gently 10 minutes.
3. Pack into hot, sterilized pint jars or half-pint jars, leaving ½ inch headspace. Wipe the rims, seal with hot lids, and firmly screw on bands. Process in a boiling water bath 15 minutes (pint jars) or 10 minutes (half-pint jars). Remove jars from canner and cool on racks.

Makes about ten cups (ten half-pint jars or five pint jars)

Crispy Thin Homemade Crackers

1¼ cups unsifted all-purpose flour
¼ cup unsifted cake flour
¾ teaspoon sugar
¾ teaspoon salt
¼ teaspoon cayenne pepper
⅛ teaspoon freshly ground black pepper
2 tablespoons extra virgin olive oil
7–8 tablespoons noncarbonated bottled water
¼ cup sesame seeds
¼ cup poppy seeds

1. Combine the flours, sugar, salt, and peppers in the bowl of a heavy-duty electric mixer fitted with a paddle attachment. On low speed, gradually add the olive oil, then 7 tablespoons water, beating until smooth and thoroughly combined. If necessary, add the additional tablespoon water. Divide the dough into 16 equal pieces, wrap them side by side in a large strip of plastic wrap and set aside at room temperature for 20 to 25 minutes. (If short on time, the dough package

may be refrigerated and rolled out the next day.) Adjust rack in lower third of oven; preheat oven to 400 degrees. Line baking sheets with parchment paper. Working with 1 piece of dough at a time, roll out on a lightly floured work surface until you have a long, thin irregular strip, about 18 inches long by 4 inches wide.

2. If using a pasta machine, dust the dough with flour and flatten it slightly. Set the pasta rollers at lowest setting and gradually increase the settings to 6 or 7, till dough is as thin as you would like.

3. If any tears occur in the dough, pinch them together, or moisten lightly with water to "glue," and continue. Gently place each sheet of dough on a baking sheet. Brush lightly with water, and sprinkle sesame and poppy seeds over the top.

4. Bake for 4 to 5 minutes, or until golden and crisp.

Yields sixteen long cracker strips.

Note: The dough for these crackers is very easy to make and work with using a pasta roller. If rolling out on the number 6 setting, the crackers may require 1 to 2 minutes additional baking time. Using the number 7 setting on your pasta machine will produce a very thin cracker. Try more cayenne or other spices for a variety of delicious crackers. I sometimes replace the sesame and poppy seeds with coarse salt.

Vegetable Medley Pizza

If you are pressed for time, use a ready-made pizza crust. But for the freshest taste nothing compares to homemade pizza dough.

1 12-ounce, room temperature pizza dough (see under The Basics)
1 8-ounce package cream cheese (regular, low-fat, or fat-free),
    room temperature
1 cup sour cream (regular, low-fat, or fat-free)
1 cup mayonnaise (regular, low-fat, or fat-free)
1 package Hidden Valley Ranch Salad Dressing and Seasoning Mix

2 cups broccoli, chopped
2 cups cauliflower, chopped
2 large carrots, grated
½ cup sliced black olives
1 cup shredded cheddar cheese (regular, low-fat, or fat-free)

1. Preheat oven to 425 degrees. Stretch room temperature pizza dough into a thin round crust and place on a cornmeal-dusted pizza pan, parchment paper, or baking sheet. Do not use a rolling pin as this will push gases out of dough.
2. Drizzle stretched pizza dough with extra virgin olive oil. Using pastry brush spread oil around dough, including edge. Bake for 8–10 minutes or until golden in color. Remove from oven and let cool completely.
3. In bowl, combine cream cheese, sour cream, mayonnaise, and dressing mix. Spread dressing mixture evenly over the cooled pizza crust.
4. Blend chopped vegetables and distribute over dressed pizza crust. Sprinkle shredded cheese and serve immediately. Wrap tightly and refrigerator any leftover pizza.

Serves eight.

ꭹ Bacon Cheeseburger Pizza

This is one of my top choices for a hearty-meal pizza, but it can be high in fat. If you are concerned about your fat intake, use ground turkey or meatless ground burger, fat-free shredded cheese, and turkey bacon. The taste is just as good as the regular or "full-fat" version. Also, if pickles aren't on your list of favorite pizza toppings, omit them. But first just try them on this pizza. They add a sour crispness that enhances the flavor, and you might find that you like them.

As with all my recipes, if you have no desire to make your own pizza dough or tomato sauce, by all means, use ready-made from your local grocer. The objective here is to create a great dish that satisfies your guests and brings out the smiles at your gathering.

1 12-ounce, room temperature pizza dough (see under The Basics)
1 tablespoon good-quality extra virgin olive oil, divided
8 ounces ground beef, ground turkey, or meatless
     ground burger, browned
1 medium red onion, chopped
Kosher or Hawaiian salt and freshly ground black pepper
12 ounces Tuscan Tomato Sauce (see under The Basics)
½ cup sliced hamburger dill pickles, drained (optional)
1 cup shredded cheddar cheese (regular, light, or fat-free)
½ cup freshly shredded mozzarella cheese
8 strips of bacon or turkey bacon

1. Preheat oven to 450 degrees. Stretch room temperature pizza dough into a thin round crust and place on a cornmeal-dusted pizza pan, parchment paper, or baking sheet. Do not use a rolling pin as this will push gases out of dough.
2. Drizzle stretched pizza dough with extra virgin olive oil. Using pastry brush spread oil around dough, including edge. Set side.
3. Drizzle a skillet with olive oil and add ground meat, onion, salt and pepper. Cook over medium heat until browned, about 8–10 minutes. Remove from heat.
4. Spread tomato sauce evenly over the pizza dough and top with browned meat.
5. Spread pickle slices and cover with shredded cheeses.
6. Slide pizza into the oven and bake for 20–30 minutes. Baking times will depend on thickness of crust and amount of toppings.
7. While pizza is baking, cook bacon until crisp. Drain on paper towel.
8. Transfer pizza to a cutting board. Slice into eight sections and garnish each slice with a strip of bacon.

Serves eight.

Are YOU a Victory Canner?

Write for Free Book to

National War Garden Commission

Washington, D.C.

Charles Lathrop Pack, President   P.S. Ridsdale, Secretary

✔ Dill Pickle Dip

Grandma used to make this dip as a treat for us grandchildren during the summer. While the rest of the family was out working on the farm, Grandma babysat my sister and me. She would let us help her mix this dip; I loved adding the dill pickle juice and stirring it in. The fragrance of this dilly dip is phenomenal. Enjoy it with regular, low-fat, or baked potato chips. As a child, my favorite indulgence was to dip dill pickle chips we could only buy on trips to Winnipeg, Manitoba. Now dill pickle chips are available everywhere. This was pure heaven with a glass of Kool-Aid. Serve the dip in a bowl on a platter or tray filled with crackers, chips, or crudités. Enjoy!

8 ounces cream cheese (regular, low-fat, or fat-free), softened
½ cup cottage cheese (regular or low-fat)
¼ cup sour cream (regular, low-fat, or fat-free)
¼ cup salad dressing (regular, light, or fat-free)
¼ cup Grandma's Sweet Cucumber Relish
    (see recipe in this chapter)
¼ cup dill pickle juice

1. Combine all ingredients in a food processor and pulse until well blended. If mixing by hand, first mash the cottage cheese with a potato masher to create a smoother dip.
2. Chill at least 1 hour before serving.

Note: I have added 2 cups of crumbled smoked salmon and spread on my Kaiser or Hamburger buns lined with lettuce for a fantastic and light (if using fat-free) lunch.

La Dolce Vita Gathering

THIS CHAPTER ENCAPSULATES a remarkable journey that started only a short time ago. At the beginning of the new millennium, I read a book titled *Under the Tuscan Sun* by Frances Mayes. It was a pleasure to read Frances's descriptions of buying and remodeling an old villa in Italy. But, at the time, living in another country didn't appeal to me and neither did traveling. My partner, Chad, spoke continuously of traveling and taking me to faraway lands full of things to discover. When I moved from the Red River Valley of North Dakota in 1997, after losing almost all of my personal belongings in the "Flood of the Century," I brought with me one possession the muddy waters couldn't alter—lessons learned from childhood. Those included not only critical food preparation methods that have served me well through the writing of this book but also the apprehension that others would harm me because I came from the "country" or from a simpler existence. Had my home, belongings, and city not been destroyed by floodwaters, I probably would have continued living in Grand Forks. The flood was the helpful boot out of the gate.

One day at the movies, I saw a preview for the film *Under the Tuscan Sun*, based on Frances Mayes's book. I thought about Chad. If we saw the movie, he could see the Italian countryside, and I wouldn't have to leave the safety of my home. So when the movie opened in the Twin Cities, we went to a matinee with my best friend, Dan Kenward.

One month before we went to the movie, a group of our friends (the Benson sisters, Lanee', Leslie, and Lorna, and our neighbor Laura McCallum) got together and planned a trip to London, England. Chad was energized by this meeting and convinced me to go along on the trip.

I said yes, but I still didn't have my passport. Secretly, I decided I wouldn't get one, and maybe he would go with our friends and I could stay home. I pretended to be interested for several weeks. Chad was the happiest I had seen him. Wanderlust was his companion now while he dreamed of the upcoming vacation. I felt guilty for my tricky plan to not obtain my passport.

As the movie started, I secretly desired that Chad's viewing a movie about someone buying a home in Italy might eradicate "Europe Lust" from his system. At the beginning of the film, the character based on Frances Mayes is deposited in Florence, Italy, at the Duomo. I thought Chad was pretending to be crying. I began to make fun of him and then noticed he was shedding real tears. That hurt me deeply because I could see how badly he wanted to experience this magnificent building in person. He even whispered that he would never get to see the Duomo. Sentiment aside, I wasn't yet moved to board an airplane to Europe.

As the film continued, we were treated to wonderful panoramas of the Tuscan countryside. And then, the title character visits Cortona, an Etruscan hill town near the eastern edge of Tuscany. I am not quite sure at what moment I was stirred, but I remember turning to Dan and whispering, "Why are we going to London?" Moments later, I whispered in Chad's ear, "Why are we not going here rather than London?" I remember posing that question several times throughout the movie. On the drive home, Chad and I talked about Italy. I had several questions but continually came back to, "Why are we not going to Italy?"

Naturally, Chad was stunned that I had become interested in traveling anywhere beyond North Dakota, Minnesota, and Wisconsin. It was as if the cosmos had cracked open for me. I was touched personally by what I witnessed on the movie screen. It was Cortona—the ancient streets through which the characters were walking and shopping—and the countryside. It was as if I had been there before and longed to return. I yearned for it. I was puzzled by my response to all this and found myself searching the Internet for lodging in Italy but especially for apartments or villas around Cortona. Ultimately, our friends were convinced to change their travel plans from London to Italy. They too were surprised by my response but eager to travel to Italy.

I feverishly worked to arrange lodging in Rome, Florence, and Venice.

I continued to search out information about Cortona and found Il Rifugio ("the refuge") a seventeenth-century stone farmhouse for rent near Cortona. I was overcome by its beauty. I shared the Web site address with our friends so that they could see photos of the farmhouse and surrounding hill towns and countryside, and we decided that we should visit it while in Italy—just in case we wanted to go back and rent it someday. So we booked a van to drive from Venice to Rome to board our flight back to the Twin Cities and planned a stop to visit Cortona and Il Rifugio.

Once the commitment was made, a great deal of activity occurred, and my life has continued to be very active. Because of Frances Mayes's tale, the movie based on her book, and her other books (*Bella Tuscany, In Tuscany,* and *Bringing Tuscany Home*), I have come to love Italy. I have now visited Cortona twice and lived at Il Rifugio for two weeks in 2005. I realized my dream of cooking in a Tuscan kitchen in an old Tuscan farmhouse. The view from the terrace was breathtaking and every evening we were treated to sunsets behind Cortona that only poets can describe. I now stroll through the Piazza della Repubblica and am greeted by friends Ivan Botantic, owner of Galeria "Il Pozzo," Marco Molesini, owner of Molesini Market and Enoteca, and Maurizio and Barbara Menci, a brother and sister who, with their parents, own Enoteca La Saletta. These are my friends on the other side of the world. They are part of the contentment that I feel when I am in Italy. We have coined the term "Cortona Coma" to describe the state that ensues after a couple of hours sitting at a sidewalk table at Enoteca La Saletta, sipping glasses of prosecco and dining on black truffle crepes. It's a magical world. (As a happy side note, Il Rifugio's owners, Chuck and Shirley Ofria, have offered me the position of a lifetime. They have asked me to teach cooking classes at Il Rifugio and bring culinary tours to their beautiful world. Check out their Web site at www.sojourn-in-italy.com, and join us for a wonderful cooking event that includes cultural and historical tours of the surrounding countryside.)

So, my life has changed dramatically because of the words of one woman. I read *Under the Tuscan Sun* again last year, for I felt I owed it another look. I paid more attention this time and it was like reading a different book, because I was a different man.

I met Frances Mayes at a reception in the Twin Cites in October

2004. The reception was exceptional, and I left inspired by the words she spoke regarding Italy and the process of a writer. I had so much I wanted to tell her but didn't want to frighten her by coming across as a fanatical groupie or fan. I wanted to explain my transformation from fearful homebody to newborn world voyager. I wrote a couple of words in a card that explained how her book had changed my life and included an invitation to Il Rifugio if she and her husband, Ed, had time to join us for a glass of wine.

Since that time I have also discovered Bramasole olive oil, which Ed and Frances Mayes produce at Villa Bramasole, the house Frances described purchasing. I use their oil exclusively in all my cooking in American and Italian cuisine. Whether for dipping my foccacia, in my Gamberi con Aglio, or for frying polenta, Bramasole olive oil is the finest oil I have ever used in my kitchen. Check out the Web site for Bramasole olive oil at www.TheTuscanSun.com. It's overflowing with extraordinary information concerning olive oils. I took pleasure in reading the "The Story of Bramasole Oil" and learning how they pick the olives by hand and "grind them without heat in the artisanal manner." What I admire most about Ed and Frances's business is that a portion of the proceeds from their olive oil sales is given to the city of Cortona for various civic improvement projects.

So, invite your family, your friends, coworkers, or anyone who is stressed from the rigors of life and work. Cook up a couple of these recipes that I have gleaned from kitchens in Rome, Florence, and Venice. Serve bottles of Italian wine and Bramasole olive oil. No television! Find a radio station with big band, swing, or jazz. Better yet, find a collection of Italian standards and play them for your guests. Don't hurry the food. Light candles, sit back, and invite everyone to gather in "the sweet life," *la dolce vita.*

"At the moment of commitment, the universe will conspire to assist you."

—JEAN-PAUL SARTRE

SUGGESTED SELECTIONS FOR YOUR LA DOLCE VITA GATHERING

- Suggested Italian Wines
    - Chianti Classico Riserva, Banfi Toscana
    - Col Di Sasso, Banfi Toscana
    - Syrah Cortona Il Bosco
- Venetian Shrimp Cocktail
- Venetian Lasagna
- Spaghetti alla Carbonara
- Meat Ragù
- Mushroom Ragù
- Gamberi alla Marinara, or Shrimp in Tuscan Tomato Sauce
- Gamberi con Aglio, or Shrimp with Garlic
- Sea Bass
- Polenta
- Fried Polenta
- Torta di Mele, or Apple Cake
- Cannoli alla Siciliana, or Dessert Cannoli

⸕ Venetian Shrimp Cocktail

This recipe is my take on the beginning of my first meal in Venice, Italy. I ordered lasagna (see the following recipe) and was convinced by the waiter to try this shrimp cocktail appetizer. Back in the United States I have not been partial to shrimp cocktail. And trust me; I've had my share, especially while visiting Las Vegas. However, this was quite different and offered such a unique taste. The little trattoria served my shrimp cocktail in a large wine goblet with a wide opening. In the bottom of the goblet was a bed of ruby red radicchio. The shrimp cocktail was served on top. I want you to try this recipe as it is so different from other shrimp cock-tails. When I found out the recipe I was quite surprised. I assumed that the ingredients were handed down from generations of Venetians and contained special and unique northern Italian herbs. I am sure I looked stunned when the list of ingredients was given to me. The owner of the trattoria glanced at me as if I had not understood his English. I had but was amazed at the simple recipe. Try it and you, too, will be astonished and, I hope, delighted.

> ½ cup tomato catsup
> 1 tablespoon Worcestershire sauce
> 1 cup mayonnaise (regular, low-fat, or fat-free)
> ¼ cup good-quality brandy
> 1 pound large shrimp, clean, deveined, with tails on

1. In a mixing bowl, combine catsup, Worcestershire sauce, mayon-naise, and brandy. Whisk together until well blended.
2. Add shrimp and gently stir to coat each shrimp with the sauce.
3. Serve in martini or champagne saucer–type glasses on a bed of radic-chio leaves with pickle spear and Italian flat leaf parsley garnish.

Serves six.

Venetian Lasagna

When I visited Venice, I tasted the most incredible lasagna. It wasn't made with ricotta cheese between its layers, as I had eaten in the United States. Instead, it was layered with a white, or béchamel, sauce. It was extraordinary. I poked my head into the kitchen and asked what the recipe was. In broken English, I was given the basic components. Once I was back home, I worked on making this my own by enhancing the white sauce with egg yolk and using my own Meat Ragù recipe. Nothing was lost in the translation, and I will always be in debt to the wonderful chef of that little trattoria we visited one chilly evening near Piazza San Marco in Venice.

1 batch of Meat Ragù (see later in this chapter)
½ cup unsalted butter
¾ cup all-purpose flour
3 cups whole milk, divided
1 bay leaf
Kosher or Hawaiian salt
Freshly ground black pepper
½ teaspoon freshly ground nutmeg
4 large egg yolks, slightly beaten
16 ounces fresh or dried lasagna
1½ cups freshly grated Parmigiano-Reggiano cheese
1¼ cups freshly grated Pecorino Romano cheese
unsalted butter

1. Prepare Meat Ragù and set aside. Spray a 13- × 9-inch oblong baking pan with cooking spray.
2. In a heavy-bottom saucepan prepare the béchamel sauce. Over low heat melt butter. Add flour and stir until well blended. Remove from heat and slowly add ⅓ of the milk. Stir until smooth and no lumps. Add bay leaf. Continue adding the rest of the milk and return to heat, stirring until sauce thickens. Remove bay leaf once sauce has thickened. Add salt, pepper, and nutmeg. Combine a small amount of the

hot sauce with the beaten egg yolks. Add egg mixture to sauce and continue cooking over low heat for additional 2 minutes. Stir continuously to prevent scorching.

3. Preheat oven to 400 degrees. Prepare pasta according to the directions on the package. Remove pasta from water 2 minutes before completely cooked for a firmer lasagna. Lay pasta on dish towels to remove excess water.

ASSEMBLY

Have all components ready. Spread ¼ cup Meat Ragù over the bottom of the baking pan. Arrange your first layer of pasta, trimming pieces to make sure they fit the pan well. Cover the pasta with a thin layer of the Meat Ragù and then with a layer of the sauce. Scatter about ¼ cup of the cheeses over the sauce. Repeat this process in order until you have three layers. End with a layer of the sauce. Scatter remaining cheeses and dot with unsalted butter.

Bake uncovered for about 20 minutes or until the cheeses have turned a golden brown. Remove from oven and let rest for 10 minutes before serving.

Serves eight to ten. Mangia!

Spaghetti alla Carbonara

As we traveled the famous cities of Italy, I made a vow to myself to try a different Italian dish at every meal. Chad, however, found one dish and ordered it six times. On New Year's Day in Rome, Lorna Benson, her sister Leslie, Chad, and I took a walk along the Tiber River. It was a beautiful sunny day with temperatures in the sixties. We stepped off the path along the river and found a small trattoria where locals eat. The owner waved us in, and I had my first taste of Spaghetti alla Carbonara. When I asked the kitchen staff what made this dish so creamy, the answer surprised me. I was instructed to add hot pasta water to the egg mixture. This cooks the eggs while it creams together the eggs and cheese. I hope you enjoy this recipe as much as Chad did during our trip to Italy!

2 tablespoons extra virgin olive oil
¼ pound unsmoked pancetta, chopped
1 large garlic clove, crushed and left in one piece
16 ounces spaghetti or fettuccini
3 large eggs, room temperature
1 cup freshly grated Parmigiano-Reggiano cheese
1 cup freshly grated Pecorino Romano cheese
Kosher or Hawaiian salt
Freshly ground black pepper
1 ladle, or 1 cup, pasta water

1. In a large stockpot or kettle, bring water to a boil. When water begins to boil, add salt.
2. Heat oil in a heavy-bottom skillet. Add pancetta and garlic. Cook until pancetta browns. Remove the garlic and discard. Set pancetta aside.
3. Add pasta to boiling water and cook following directions on package or until *al dente* if using fresh pasta.

Note: Al dente is an Italian phrase for pasta that's fully cooked but not too soft. The phrase literally means "to the tooth," which comes from testing the pasta's consistency by biting it. When pasta is cooked al dente, there should be a slight resistance in the center when the pasta is chewed.

4. While pasta is boiling, break eggs in a large, heat-resistant bowl. Place over boiling pasta water and stir until very warm. Remove from heat and stir in cheeses. Season with salt and pepper. Pour pasta water over egg mixture and blend in.
5. Drain pasta and mix with egg mixture. Add pancetta and its hot oil. Combine.

Serves six.

Meat Ragù

2 tablespoons unsalted butter
2 tablespoons extra virgin olive oil
¾ cup yellow onion, chopped
2 tablespoons pancetta, unsmoked
1 large carrot, thinly sliced
1 celery stalk, thinly sliced
1 large garlic clove, minced
1 pound lean ground beef or ground turkey
Kosher or Hawaiian salt
Freshly ground black pepper
¾ cup red wine
½ cup milk (regular or vanilla soy)
2 cups roma tomatoes, chopped with juice
   (see Canned Roma Tomatoes under The Basics)
1 bay leaf
½ teaspoon fresh English or French thyme

1. In a heavy-bottom saucepan, melt butter. Stir in oil and onion. Cook over medium heat until onion is translucent. Add pancetta and cook until it begins to crisp. Blend in carrot, celery, and garlic and cook until tender, about 8 minutes.
2. Crumble in ground meat. Cook until browned. Season with salt and pepper. Add wine, turn up heat to medium-high, and cook until the liquid evaporates, about 15 minutes.
3. Pour tomatoes into meat mixture. Stir in herbs and bring to a boil. Turn heat to low and simmer, uncovered, for 2 hours. Stir ragù occasionally until glossy and resembles a meaty jeweled sauce.

Note: Serve both Meat Ragù and Mushroom Ragù with spaghetti, fettuccine, farfalle, rigatoni, fusilli, or penne pastas. Be creative, but use these sauces in a variety of ways from filling for lasagna, topping for polenta, or a simple pasta sauce.

Serves eight to ten.

⨍ Mushroom Ragù

If fresh mushrooms are difficult to find in your area, you can substitute dried but reconstitute them first by pouring boiling water over the dried mushrooms, filling a container halfway. Cover it to trap the steam and steep 5 to 10 minutes or until mushrooms are tender. Do not discard the mushroom liquid. To add extra flavor, replace ½ cup of the chicken broth with mushroom water for a more "shroomy" flavor.

For an entirely new Venetian Lasagna replace the Meat Ragù with this recipe. Serve both the Meat Ragù lasagna and Mushroom Ragù lasagne to please both your carnivore and your vegetarian guests.

> ¼ cup extra virgin olive oil
> 1 large onion (I prefer Vidalia if available), chopped
> 2 large garlic cloves, minced
> 16 ounces mushrooms (button, cepe/porcini, chanterelle, cremini, morel, oyster, shitake, and wood ear)
> Kosher or Hawaiian salt
> Freshly ground black pepper
> ½ cup good quality Marsala wine
> 2 cups chicken broth, low sodium
> ⅓ cup heavy cream or fat-free half-and-half
> ⅓ cup Italian flat-leaf parsley, chopped
> 2 sprigs fresh rosemary, finely chopped
> ½ cup freshly grated Parmigiano-Reggiano cheese
> ½ cup freshly grated Pecorino Romano cheese

1. In a heavy-bottom skillet over medium heat, cook garlic in oil but do not brown or garlic will become bitter. Add onion and cook until translucent.
2. Combine mushrooms with onion and garlic. Season with salt and pepper. Continue cooking until liquid evaporates.
3. Remove mushroom mixture from heat and stir in Marsala. Return to heat and cook, stirring occasionally, until liquid evaporates again.

4. Turn heat to low and add chicken broth. Simmer, uncovered, for 45 minutes to 1 hour or until the sauce has reduced in volume by half.
5. Blend in cream. Remove from heat and combine herbs and cheeses into the sauce.

Serves eight to ten.

⸓ Gamberi alla Marinara, or Shrimp in Tuscan Tomato Sauce

Serve this sauce with cold polenta or fried polenta. I've served it over cooked pasta accompanied with roasted garlic bread, but this dish is fantastic simply on its own. That is how Gamberi alla Marinara was served to me the first time I experienced it on New Year's Day. Our good friend Laura McCallum joined our group after an all-night New Year's Eve flight from Minneapolis to Rome. Seven of us descended on Ristorante Marcello to celebrate that we were all together on New Year's Day.

      1 tablespoon extra virgin olive oil
      3 large garlic cloves, minced
      3 tablespoons fresh Italian flat-leaf parsley, chopped
      ¼ teaspoon red pepper flakes
      1 recipe Tuscan Tomato Sauce (see under The Basics)
      Kosher or Hawaiian salt
      Freshly ground black pepper
      2 pounds fresh shrimp, peeled, deveined, with tails on

1. In a large heavy-bottom saucepan, heat oil over medium heat. Add garlic, parsley, and red pepper flakes. Cook, stirring constantly so that garlic does not burn and turn bitter. Garlic should be golden.
2. Add Tuscan Tomato Sauce and bring to a boil, stirring occasionally. Season with salt and pepper.
3. Add shrimp and bring back to a boil. Reduce heat to low and simmer until shrimp turn pink. Remove from heat and serve.

Serves eight to ten.

ƒ Gamberi con Aglio, or Shrimp with Garlic

This recipe is a fine example of how a good quality extra virgin olive oil, such as Bramasole Olive Oil, enhances the taste of the dish.

⅓ cup extra virgin olive oil
4 large garlic cloves, minced
1 cup Italian bread crumbs
½ teaspoon fresh oregano, chopped
¼ cup Italian flat-leaf parsley, chopped
2 pounds medium or large shrimp, peeled, deveined, with tails on
Kosher or Hawaiian salt
Freshly ground black pepper
1 tablespoon fresh basil, cut into thin strips

1. Preheat oven to 450 degrees. Spray a 13- × 9-inch oblong baking pan with cooking spray or wipe with olive oil. Set aside.
2. In a mixing bowl, combine olive oil, garlic, bread crumbs, oregano, and parsley. Place the shrimp, in a single layer, in the baking pan. Sprinkle bread crumb-herb mixture over shrimp. Splash additional olive oil over crumb mixture and season with salt and pepper.
3. Bake for 10 minutes or until crumb mixture browns and shrimp become pink. Remove and scatter basil on top before serving. Do not bake basil as it will turn black.

Serves eight to ten.

"The watering of a garden requires as much judgment as the seasoning of a soup."

—Helena Rutherford Ely

∤ Sea Bass

After a long day exploring the treasures of Florence, we crossed the Ponte Vecchio and found a ristorante overlooking the Arno River. We arrived around 6:00 p.m., ready for supper. The staff sat us at a table with a river view but explained the kitchen would not serve until 7:00 p.m., as is the Italian fashion. We ordered cocktails and wine and enjoyed the view. Several tables over, a large group or family was also having drinks before dinner and enjoying each other's company. Seven o'clock arrived and we ordered. I chose this superb sea bass and a martini. We enjoyed dessert and prepared to leave. It felt as if we had spent the entire evening but I was jolted back into reality when I noticed that the large group a few tables away were just now ordering their first course, *primi piatti-pasta*. How quickly we ate was another sure sign that we were not from Italy.

1 sea bass, approximately 3 pounds, scaled and gutted
3 large garlic cloves, minced
1 tablespoon Italian flat-leaf parsley, chopped
1 tablespoon fresh rosemary, chopped
1 sprig of fresh English or French thyme leafs
1 lemon, thinly sliced
½ teaspoon kosher or Hawaiian salt
¼ freshly ground black pepper
¼ cup extra virgin olive oil

1. Preheat the oven to 400 degrees. Place a large piece of aluminum foil, enough to fold around the sea bass, on a baking sheet. Set aside.
2. Rinse and dry cleaned fish. In a small bowl, combine garlic, parsley, rosemary, thyme, salt, and pepper. Fill fish cavity with almost all the herb mixture, packing gill and belly areas. Save some of the herb mixture to sprinkle on the outside of the fish. Place lemon slices along belly area from head to tail, showing rind along cut in belly.

3. After placing sea bass on foil-covered baking sheet, dash with olive oil and sprinkle with remaining herb mixture. Fold and seal the fish in foil. Bake for 30 minutes. Remove from oven and place in a serving dish still wrapped in foil.

Serves two.

⨎ Polenta

The preparation of polenta takes strong arms. You must continually stir the polenta until it is done. It becomes as thick as cement but is a wonderful addition to any Italian menu.

  4 cups water
  1½ teaspoons kosher or Hawaiian salt
  1 cup polenta or coarse-grain yellow cornmeal
  2 tablespoons unsalted butter

In a heavy-bottom stockpot or Dutch oven, bring water to a boil over medium heat. Add salt. Pour polenta into boiling water and stir constantly until thickened, about 30 minutes. Add butter and blend in. When polenta begins to withdraw from the sides of the pot, it is ready. You will need to continuously stir, preferably with a wooden spoon. Pour into bowl and let cool to room temperature. The polenta should be firm. Turn out of bowl. Serve to guests topped with Meat or Mushroom Ragù or cut into pieces and let your guests add their own topping.

Serves six.

⸘ Fried Polenta

    1 recipe of polenta, firm and at room temperature
    ¼ cup extra virgin olive oil

1. In a heavy-bottom skillet, heat oil.
2. Slice polenta into ½-inch-thick pieces. Fry a few pieces at a time in hot oil. Season with salt and pepper, if desired.
3. Serve plain or with favorite topping, such as Meat or Mushroom Ragù.

⸘ Torta di Mele, or Apple Cake

    1 cup olive oil (I have used vegetable oil, but olive oil gives this cake
        a true Italian heart.)
    1 cup dark brown sugar
    1 cup superfine baker's sugar
    2 large eggs, slightly beaten
    2 cups all-purpose flour
    1 cup golden raisins
    1 cup pecans, chopped
    1 teaspoon baking soda
    1 teaspoon kosher or Hawaiian salt
    2 teaspoons cinnamon
    1 teaspoon pure vanilla extract
    4 cups Golden Delicious or Granny Smith apples, unpeeled, cored,
        and thinly sliced

"Tickle the earth with a hoe, it will laugh a harvest."

—AUTHOR UNKNOWN

1. Preheat oven to 350 degrees. Spray 9-inch springform, tube, or Bundt pan with cooking spray. Line bottom of springform pan with parchment paper.
2. Combine oil, sugars, and eggs. Stir in flour, raisins, pecans, soda, salt, cinnamon, and vanilla. Gently fold in the sliced apples. This batter is extremely thick and lumpy. It is not smooth as are most cake batters. Do not be alarmed.
3. Spoon batter into prepared pan and bake for 90 minutes or until a skewer inserted comes out clean.
4. Remove from oven and cool on wire rack for 10 minutes. Turn out cake onto serving plate and sprinkle with superfine baker's or vanilla sugar. Serve warm.
5. Top with Caramel Sauce or Sweetened Whipped Cream (see both under The Basics).

Serves eight to ten.

⸙ Cannoli alla Siciliana, or Dessert Cannoli

I was introduced to this magnificent dessert at Ristorante "Aurora 10" our first night in Rome. Leslie Benson, Chad, and I continued exploring the city after the rest of our group returned to the hotel. Leslie and I discussed the insignificance of several matters in our lives that made living complicated. Rome does this to visitors. After our delicious meal, our waiter tempted us with desserts. He insisted that we try the Cannoli alla Siciliana, or Sicilian-style fritters, with our coffee. Wow! An extremely simple dessert, it was creamy, crunchy, sweet, fruity, and full of chocolate. I was in heaven. It set the tone for the remainder of our trip through Italy.

You could prepare your own cannoli shells and that is probably best, but Italian specialty stores carry hand-rolled shells, and isn't it all about living *la dolce vita*? Make sure your ricotta is extremely fresh. This recipe does not transfer well to low-fat or fat-free, so go for broke.

2 cups or 1 pound whole milk ricotta, preferably ewe's milk ricotta
1⅓ cups superfine baker's sugar or ½ cup confectioner's sugar
1 cup candied orange, cherries, and/or dried berry mix, chopped
1 cup chocolate chips, chopped
¼ teaspoon cinnamon
8 to 10 cannoli shells
Confectioner's sugar for sprinkling

1. In a mixing bowl, combine ricotta and sugar until well blended. Add candied fruit, chocolate chips, and cinnamon.
2. Just before serving, use a pastry bag or spoon to fill cannoli shells with ricotta mixture. Decorate ends of filled shells with whole candied fruit and additional chocolate chips. Sprinkle with confectioner's sugar.

Serves eight to ten.

"The sun, with all those planets revolving around it and dependent upon it, can still ripen a bunch of grapes as if it had nothing else in the universe to do."

—GALILEO

The Basics

*I*HAVE TURNED almost our entire backyard into garden space for berries, vegetables, and herbs. Having had the good fortune to grow up on a farm in North Dakota, I learned how to garden and preserve food at a young age. I helped Grandma prepare food for the hired hands who traveled to the Red River Valley each year to plant and harvest our fields. I learned from an early age how to cook for a crowd, how to be frugal, how to be creative, and, most important, how food brought us together; it held the farm and everyone on it together. We had a happy crew tending to our farm, and that was because of Grandma's incredible cooking. When we had family gatherings for Memorial Day, the Fourth of July, and Labor Day, we also invited the hired men. They were family, too. When we cooked, everyone was invited. I was fortunate to learn how to make basic foods from the crops we grew.

It's a new millennium now. Not everyone has the time or inclination to grow food and preserve it. That's okay. I offer these recipes as a gift to you just as my grandma gave them to me. Using a bottle of pesto from the grocery store, buying breads or rolls from a bakery, or using frozen dough is not a crime. I actually love shortcuts. I use buttermilk biscuits in a paper tube— the kind you open by banging it on the edge of the countertop—and brush them with melted butter mixed with garlic powder to create garlic buttermilk biscuits. One day, a neighbor found out my secret. I say, "So what?" If something store-bought or ready-made tastes better than what I can make from scratch, why not? Taking pleasure in a gathering with your extended family and friends does not require blood, sweat, and tears over an oppressive stove. It involves good listening skills, conversation, and laughter. It also calls for a tall cool beverage with a multicolored paper umbrella in it.

BASIC COMPONENTS FOR GARDEN COUNTY RECIPES

- Apple Butter
- Basil Pesto and variations
- Chicken Broth
- Sponge
- Hamburger Buns
- Pizza/Focaccia Dough
- Tuscan Tomato Sauce
- Canned Roma Tomatoes
- Simple Dill Sauce
- Dill Sauce
- Caramel Sauce
- Sweetened Whipped Cream
- Cocktails—The Basics
- Sour Mix
- Equivalents

Apple Butter

2001 Winner, Second Place Apple Butter, Minnesota State Fair

This recipe has been in the family for generations, and I am very proud of it. It involves a good deal of manual labor but is well worth it. The treasure you receive as you open a jar of this aromatic preserve will enliven your senses. Sample it on toast, in my Apple Butter Hand Pies (see under American Pie Festival Gathering), or on your morning oatmeal.

6 pounds cooking apples, cut into quarters,
      seeded but leave skins on
4 cups fresh apple cider, not from concentrate
2½ cups dark brown sugar
2 teaspoons cinnamon
½ teaspoon allspice
¼ teaspoon cloves
¼ teaspoon kosher or Hawaiian salt
1 fresh lemon, juiced and strained

1. In a 12-quart heavy-bottom stockpot, heat apples and cider over high heat. Bring to a boil and hard boil for 5 minutes. Reduce heat to medium, cover, and continue cooking until apples are soft, approximately 45 minutes, stirring occasionally to prevent scorching.

2. Remove apples from heat and process through a food mill or sieve. Mill pulp into a large nonmetal bowl. Discard peels into your compost. Carefully pour milled apple pulp back into the stockpot and add sugar, cinnamon, allspice, cloves, salt, and lemon juice. Stir well to combine.

3. Reduce heat to low and simmer for about 2 hours, stirring frequently to prevent scorching. I suggest pulling up a bar stool for your comfort. (*Note:* Be careful. This mixture will bubble and spatter as it thickens.) With a long handle wooden spoon in pot, place the stockpot cover over pot but leaving open enough space allowed by the spoon handle. Stir gently before removing the pot cover to stir down hot mixture.

4. When mixture has reduced by half, thickened, and mounds when dropped from your stirring spoon, it is finished cooking. Prepare canning jars according to manufacture's instructions. Fill sterilized half-pint jars with hot mixture, leaving ½-inch headspace. Process in a boiling-water canner for 10 minutes. Cool on towel or rack. Test to make sure seal is set.

Makes ten to twelve half-pint jars.
May store up to two years in a cool, dry, and dark area.

⸀ Basil Pesto

2 "packed" cups fresh basil leaves; Genovese or
  Sicilian is recommended
2 garlic gloves
½ cup freshly grated Parmigiano-Reggiano cheese
⅛ cup freshly grated Pecorino Romano cheese
¼ cup toasted pine nuts
¼ teaspoon kosher or Hawaiian salt
½ cup extra virgin olive oil
Freshly ground pepper

1. Preheat oven to 350 degrees. Distribute the pine nuts on a baking sheet and toast until golden, stirring once, about 10 minutes. Cool before mixing into pesto.
2. In food processor, pulse basil, garlic, cheeses, pine nuts, and salt until finely chopped. With the food processor running, add olive oil in a slow, steady stream until well blended. Pesto should be the consistency of an emulsified paste. Season with pepper. Let stand 5–10 minutes for flavors to relax.
3. Toss with fresh or dried pasta, spread on toasted bread squares or crackers, or use in appetizers such as Pesto Cheese Ball with Sun-Dried Tomatoes (see under The Academy Awards Gathering).

Time-Saving Tip: I pick large quantities of fresh basil from my garden and replant halfway through the season for a continued harvest. This allows me to process several batches of pesto, which I place in ice cube trays and freeze. Once the cubes are frozen, I release them from the trays, vacuum pack, and freeze for later use. You can also use freezer bags that zip shut. When you want fresh pesto, simply remove the desired amount and thaw. One quick tip is to prepare and drain fresh or dried pasta, and add frozen pesto cubes. The heat from the drained pasta will thaw the pesto. Toss and serve for a delicious burst of summer garden flavor.

Variations: I grow many varieties of herbs in my garden and like to create distinctive pesto experiences. For Basil-Chive Pesto, use 1½ cups basil and ½ cup chives. For Oregano Pesto, 1 cup Italian oregano and 1 cup fresh Italian flat-leaf parsley. For Sage Pesto, 1 cup fresh sage and 1 cup Italian flat-leaf parsley. For Rosemary Pesto, 1 cup fresh rosemary leaves and 1 cup fresh Italian flat-leaf parsley. You get the idea. Try your own combinations with other herbs such as French tarragon, English thyme, and so many other wonderful and aromatic herbs.

⨍ Chicken Broth

Making your own broth is very simple and allows you to work on other things around your home while it's stewing. I use chicken broth in my Asian dishes (see Chicken Asparagus or Stir-Fried Rice under Gathering at Mokihana on the Island of Kauai) to create my cooking sauce or in place of water to add more flavor to a variety of recipes. Of course, the best use is for my Chicken Noodle Soup (see under Housewarming Gathering).

   1 5-pound whole chicken or pieces
   3 quarts water
   2 14-ounce cans low-sodium, low-fat chicken broth
   9 black, white, green peppercorns (3 of each)
   3 bay leaves
   1 large onion, cut into quarters
   3 carrots, chopped
   2 celery stalks, chopped
   3 green onions with greens, chopped
   ⅓ cup fresh dill, chopped
   ⅓ cup fresh Italian flat-leaf parsley, chopped

1. In an 8- or 12-quart stockpot over medium-high heat, cover chicken with water and chicken broth. Bring to a boil. Add peppercorns, bay leaves, onion, carrots, celery, green onions, dill, and parsley. Reduce heat until bubbles just rise to the top of broth. Cover and simmer for 1 hour.
2. Remove chicken from the stockpot and, when cool enough to handle, remove meat from bones. Cut meat into bite-sized chunks and let cool before refrigerating. Return bones to the stock pot.
3. Continue to simmer broth for an additional 3 hours. Make sure that bubbles are just rising, slowly, to the top of the broth.
4. Strain broth through a fine-mesh sieve or through a double layer of cheesecloth. Let broth cool to room temperature.
5. Store in jars in the refrigerator for up to three days. May be frozen in storage bags or vacuum bags up to four months. Make sure to label with date before storing.

Note: For a broth without meat, I save chicken bones from previous meals and freeze them in storage bags. When I have 2 pounds of bones, I will prepare my broth. I also save the rough rinds from cheese such as Parmigiano-Reggiano and Pecorino Romano. I freeze in storage bags and add 1 cup of the cheese rinds to my broth when I add the chicken bones.

⸖ Sponge

Grandma taught me to begin the dough-making process by starting a "sponge," or what others call a "poolish"—a yeast-based mixture—hours before the dough is actually formed. Sponge creates a rich flavor, wonderfully dense texture, and delicious yeasty aroma. I begin this process the day before I plan to make bread, buns, rolls, or pizza/focaccia dough. If you use this for bread, buns, or rolls, replace 1 cup water in the recipe with 1 cup sponge.

2 cups unbleached white flour
2 cups water
¼ teaspoon yeast

In a large container with a secure lid, combine flour, water, and yeast. With whisk or fork, mix until well blended. Cover and set in a cool dark area. Bubbles will begin to appear after several hours, signaling that the fermentation process is under way. At this point, usually 4 hours, you may refrigerate if you are not planning to use until the next day.

Note: I start my sponge before I go to bed. It is ready for me to use the next morning. In warmer climates, this mixture will begin to ferment quickly. I made a container of sponge while staying on the island of Kauai for a week. Before going to bed, I immediately placed the container in the refrigerator and the next morning the sponge was pushing the top off the container. Heat and humidity make this mixture react rather quickly.

⸕ Hamburger Buns

2 tablespoons active dry yeast
8 cups all-purpose flour, divided
2 cups warm water
¾ cup vegetable or extra virgin olive oil; taste will vary
    according to the oil you use
½ cup sugar
1 tablespoon kosher or Hawaiian salt
3 large eggs

1. Combine yeast and 4 cups of flour in a large mixing bowl using a bread whisk or wooden spoon.
2. Blend together water, oil, sugar, and salt. Add to flour mixture. Stir until well blended. Add eggs and beat with bread whisk or spoon until

well incorporated. Using your hands, mix in remaining flour to make soft dough.

3. Turn mixture out onto a lightly floured surface and begin kneading the dough until smooth and elastic, about 10 minutes. Add flour only as needed to prevent dough being sticky. You should be able to press your finger anywhere in the dough and it will bounce back immediately.

4. Spray a clean large bowl with cooking spray. Place dough in bowl. Cover with a dish towel and let rise until doubled in size, about 1 to 2 hours.

5. Punch dough down. With lightly floured hands, divide dough into three portions. Cover and let rest for 10 minutes. Divide each portion into eight equal-sized pieces. Shape each piece into a ball and slightly flatten. Place on baking pans lined with Silpat liners, lightly floured parchment paper, or sprayed with cooking spray. Cover with dish towels and let rise until doubled, about 45 minutes.

6. 30 minutes before dough is ready, preheat oven to 375 degrees. Add a pan of hot water on the lowest rack to create steam while rolls bake.

7. Bake for 30 minutes until golden brown and tapping the top of the bread produces a hollow thud. Remove from pans and cool on racks.

Yields twenty-four buns.

Note: Grandma would brush melted shortening on top of each bun before baking to produce a glossy shine.

⨍ Pizza/Focaccia Dough

4 cups unbleached white flour
¾ teaspoons active dry yeast
2½ teaspoons kosher or Hawaiian salt
½–1 cups water
2 cups sponge

1. Place sponge in a large mixing bowl; add flour, yeast, and salt. Add water (start with a smaller amount and add as needed) and mix until dry ingredients are incorporated.
2. Turn mixture out onto a lightly floured surface and begin kneading until a developed dough forms, about 10 minutes.
3. Place dough in a clean oiled bowl, cover, and let rise until doubled in a warm area of your kitchen for about 2 hours.
4. Punch down dough, empty onto workspace, and fold over and punch down again. Place back in bowl, cover, and let rise 1 more hour.
5. Divide dough into ideal size for your gathering:
   * 6-ounce pizzas: divide into 8 pieces
   * 12-ounce pizzas: divide into 4 pieces
   * 1-pound focaccia or deep-dish pizza, divide into 3 pieces
6. Mound the dough into balls. Place on floured baking sheets, cover with plastic, and refrigerate 2 hours or overnight. To freeze, dust the dough balls with flour (this will help them not stick) and wrap in plastic. To thaw, let sit in the refrigerator overnight.
7. When prepared to make pizza, bring dough to room temperature. If dough is cold, large bubbles will form while in the oven and you may lose pizza toppings in your oven.

⸖ Tuscan Tomato Sauce

I cannot recommend this recipe enough. It is so fresh and full of flavor, especially if you use your own homegrown tomatoes. I can around fifty pounds of meaty roma tomatoes each year. If you don't have the desire to can your own, use the best-quality canned tomatoes you can find. With all the interest in Italian foods, you should not have any difficulty finding roma tomatoes at your local grocery store.

¼ cup extra virgin olive oil
4 large garlic cloves, minced
12 cups canned roma tomatoes (see following recipe)
1 teaspoon red pepper flakes
1 cup Chianti or other good-quality red wine
1 tablespoon fresh oregano, chopped
¼ teaspoon kosher or Hawaiian salt
⅓ teaspoon freshly ground black pepper
½ cup fresh basil leaves, torn into thin strips
½ teaspoon fresh English or French thyme leaves

1. In batches, puree tomatoes in a blender. You want your tomatoes somewhat chunky, so pulse the blender to prevent them from liquefying.
2. Using a medium-size stockpot or Dutch oven, heat the olive oil over medium heat. Add the garlic and cook until golden; do not let garlic brown as it will become bitter. Add tomatoes, red pepper flakes, and wine and reduce heat to low. While mixture is simmering, add oregano, salt, and pepper. Simmer uncovered until the sauce thickens, about 1½ to 2 hours, stirring occasionally.

---

*"In Florence you think, in Rome you pray, and in Venice you love.
In all three you eat."*

—ITALIAN PROVERB

3. Before serving, add basil and thyme and combine. Serve over fresh pasta, on pizza, or in dishes that require tomato sauce. This sauce may be kept in the refrigerator for up to five days in an airtight container. You may also freeze up to two months. I use a food vacuum and store in mason jars or freezer bags for best storage and freshness.

⸎ Canned Roma Tomatoes

I adore tomatoes and cultivate different varieties. You will always find quite a few roma plants in my garden each growing season. For making sauces, no other tomato can produce the rich, thick red sauce that comes from this variety. If you cannot grow your own romas, check at your local farmers' market. Last year, I produced around forty to fifty pounds of my own romas, but I also purchased two bushels at the Saint Paul Farmers' Market because I actually use that many tomatoes throughout the year. When canning, always pick firm, bright red tomatoes that have been freshly picked. As with all canning, please read the recipe carefully and review USDA safety instructions for preserving food.*

> 21 pounds fresh roma tomatoes, no blemishes
> 3 large bunches fresh basil, washed and dried
> Kosher or canning salt
> 7 quart or 14 pint canning jars with lids, sterilized according to
>   manufacturer's directions

1. Wash tomatoes and discard any that are bruised or blemished. Completely drain and dry tomatoes.
2. Place a couple of basil leaves on the bottom of each jar.
3. With a sharp knife, slice tomatoes in half lengthwise. Remove core and seeds. Do not peel. Place sliced side down in jars. When jar is half full, place a couple more basil leaves on top of tomatoes.

4. Continue to fill jars, pushing with back of wooden spoon to remove air bubbles. Do not apply a great deal of pressure or you may break the tomato skins. Damaging the skins is not a disaster, but it is desirable to leave tomato halves intact.

5. Fill jars to the top, leaving ¾-inch head space. Sprinkle filled jars with kosher or canning salt to prevent a skin forming. Wipe the jar rims and threads with a clean, damp cloth. Cover with hot lids and apply screw rings.

6. Place in a large water bath canner with sponges or kitchen towels between jars to prevent movement and jars rubbing against each other. Cover jars with at least one inch of water at all times, adding as necessary.

7. Process in a 200-degree water bath over medium heat for 1 hour and 15 minutes. Remove jars from canner and place on racks or thick towels. Keep out of cool drafts. Bring to room temperature.

8. Test seal. Use immediately or discard any jars that did not seal. Label and store in a cool, dry, dark area.

Makes seven quarts or fourteen pints.

Important: Before attempting to can or preserve please read carefully all USDA safety instructions for preserving food. You may view the *USDA Complete Guide to Home Canning* at: http://edis.ifas.ufl.edu/TOPIC_Canning_Food or http://foodsafety.cas.psu.edu/canningguide.html.

ƒ Simple Dill Sauce

½ cup sour cream (regular, low-fat, or fat-free)
½ cup mayonnaise (regular, low-fat, or fat-free)
1 tablespoon freshly squeezed lemon juice
1 tablespoon fresh dill, finely chopped

Combine sour cream, mayonnaise, lemon juice, and dill. Whisk together and chill for at least 1 hour before serving.

ƒ Dill Sauce

2 tablespoons unsalted butter
2 tablespoons all-purpose flour
1 cup whole milk
Dash of kosher or Hawaiian salt
Dash of freshly ground black pepper
1 teaspoon fresh dill, finely chopped

1. In a heavy-bottom saucepan melt butter over low heat. Add flour and whisk until well blended.
2. Add milk while whisking flour mixture. Continue to stir until sauce thickens. Add salt, pepper, and dill. Simmer for 5 minutes, constantly stirring. Remove from heat and serve immediately.

⸙ Caramel Sauce

8 tablespoons unsalted butter
2 tablespoons milk
1 cup dark brown sugar
3–5 tablespoons confectioner's sugar

1. In a heavy-bottom saucepan over low heat, melt butter. Add milk and brown sugar. Stir until well blended and sugar dissolves.
2. Begin adding confectioner's sugar by the spoonful, whisking until well incorporated. Continue adding until desired consistency is reached. Use less to create a sauce that will drizzle or add more for a frosting-like consistency.

⸙ Sweetened Whipped Cream

1 cup heavy or gourmet whipping cream
4 tablespoons confectioner's sugar
1 teaspoon pure vanilla extract

1. In a chilled mixing bowl and using a chilled whisk or beaters, whip cream.
2. Gradually add confectioner's sugar. Continue until stiff peaks form. Add vanilla and beat until incorporated into whipped cream.
3. Serve on pies, cakes, bars, or my Torte Di Mele, or Apple Cake (see under La Dolce Vita Gathering).

ᶠ Cocktails—The Basics

What Is a Cocktail?

Cocktails were first introduced by American bartenders in the early 1920s. During Prohibition the quality of bootleg alcohol was suspect at best and tasted likewise. Bartenders began to mix the alcohol with a variety of fruit juices and other flavors to make it more palatable. During the 1950s and 1960s, cocktails were the fashion, and a new series of cocktails drinks, foods, and music was born.

Today there is a resurgence of the cocktail craze. Ultra lounges are creating new cocktails for a new crowd. Cocktail hours and parties have entire books devoted to giving the perfect gathering, and lifestyle stores are offering a variety of mixers, shakers, swizzle sticks, and partyware. Barware has become an important part of kitchenware.

With all the flash and flair of cocktail parties and cocktail hours, who really understands what a cocktail is? Not that a recipe is required for creating the perfect cocktail, but when I first began entertaining I had no concept what mixing a drink involved. Hopefully this section will answer any questions about cocktails.

These are the basics. What could be more satisfying than having the knowledge to make a great drink even better? So take what you need from this section to enhance gatherings that will be not only memorable but stimulating.

Cocktails usually consist of four varied ingredients:

- The *foundation* is often a spirit such as vodka, rum, gin, whiskey, or tequila. Occasionally, wine may be used as a foundation for refreshing punches.

- *Flavoring* is added to bring out the aroma of the foundation and to adjust its taste. Flavoring may consist of vermouth, various fruit juices, wine, or even eggs or cream.

- *Special flavoring* is added to enhance the taste of the foundation and often adds color to the cocktail. Common special flavorings include grenadine and blue curaçao.

- *Decoration,* of course, is an integral ingredient as style is a major component to successful gatherings. Many cocktails are decorated with fruit slices, orange peel, cocktail sticks, mint sprigs, olives, paper umbrellas, and many other tasteful embellishments.

Equipment

Visit any lifestyle store within ten miles of your home and you may become overwhelmed by the many unusual contraptions that have been manufactured for the making of cocktails. Many are useful, but some are merely decorations for your bar or bar cart. I spoke with my favorite bartenders to get the right information, and not one bar item that I have purchased in the past ten years has been sold at a garage sale or donated to Goodwill.

The first piece of equipment to look for, as in any cooking, is a good-quality measuring device. In the cocktail world, measuring devices are known as jiggers. Jiggers are often made of metal, but I own a glass one. Jiggers are approximately 1 fluid ounce. Most recipes will call for 2 jiggers or 2 ounces of spirits.

The second piece of equipment you need is a cocktail shaker. I have known many people who prefer to insert one smaller glass into a larger glass and shake them, but that is simply not how it should be done. I prefer the European cocktail shaker, which is made of metal or glass. The container, which holds about half a liter of liquid, is topped by a strainer and covered by a tight-fitting cover or nose cone. Having a shaker with a strainer creates perfect cocktails.

The third piece of essential equipment is a corkscrew for wine. It is the perfect host or hostess gift. I have recently examined corkscrews that I believe to be designed by NASA. Find one that is simple but sturdy. I purchased a corkscrew that screws down into the cork as its two handles raise upward. When the screw is secure in the cork, the handles are pressed back down and the cork is lifted out. I have yet to leave any pieces of cork floating in any of my wines thanks to this excellent design.

Optional equipment, such as a blender, is important for preparing iced drinks like my Frozen Whiskey Sours or Frozen Midori Sours. Also, appealing embellishments along the lines of swizzle sticks, stirrers, extravagant napkins, straws, toothpicks for cocktail foods, and wine charms may be purchased if you desire.

Before your next gathering ask a couple of friends to join you on a shopping excursion for cocktail equipment and embellishments. Make a lunch date out of it and have a cocktail to celebrate.

Glassware

Let's start with my favorite glass—the champagne glass. The more familiar champagne flute is a tall, narrow glass with a stem. These are very elegant and made of thin glass that may be frosted or ringed with gold or silver. The type of champagne glass that I prefer is the broader champagne saucer. Because of this glass's shape, champagne loses its fizz rather quickly. However, my champagne has not lasted long enough to lose its fizz. I also use the champagne saucer for desserts or appetizers like my Venetian Shrimp Cocktail (see under La Dolce Vita Gathering).

My second favorite glass is the martini glass. These are classic cocktail glasses that make a Y-shape when viewed from the side. Many older neon signs from cocktail lounges used the martini glass as a representation of their fashionable standing. What would the cosmopolitan be without this elegant glass?

Highball glasses are usually tall with straight sides. They are used for tall or long drinks, such as a Tom Collins, or when you request a bourbon ginger ale tall. Rock glasses, also known as tumblers, are usually short and broad. Bars may also use exclusive glasses for special drinks such as a Piña Colada, Lava Flow, or Mai Tai. There are also margarita glasses or fishbowls.

I have never been controlled by the standards of which drink to serve in what glass. Have some fun and create something totally new, something that will result in a smile on your guest's face. However you serve your cocktails, please do not serve drinks in plastic. For one thing, your drink will take on the taste of plastic. Given the discount, outlet, and thrift stores available now, using genuine glassware can be economical, and ending up with a variety of styles just adds to the fun.

Mixing

This task I relinquish to the professionals. Check out your local bookstore and purchase a guide for bartenders. You will never regret this purchase. It will also help you design drink menus or cocktail party themes when you discover what interesting cocktail recipes are out there. For me, mixing consists of stirring, blending, or shaking. This is an art that is open to everyone, but you must do your homework.

Embellishment

Nothing is as boring as a cocktail in a plain glass with only ice as embellishment. My best friend, Dan Kenward, taught me years ago that even a can of beer could hold a paper umbrella. I used that knowledge and twisted my first lemon and lime peel. I speared cherries and rubbed mint leaves along the rim of a glass. In our early college years, Dan and I amused guests at gatherings, at the lake, or at parks while we sipped our beer through silly straws. He taught me to expand my ideas about cocktails.

When guests arrive, I enjoy providing refreshments that surprise but also invigorate them. Your guests will delight in the fresh mint aroma when you serve them my Nuclear Long Island Teas in glasses with rims you've rubbed with fresh mint.

When you come across a gift store that offers unique cocktail sticks, spears, straws, or other sorts of decorations, go ahead and purchase them. I have too often remembered a distinctive embellishment and wished I had bought it.

Set out bowls of twisted citrus peels, cherries, fruit slices, spiced sugars, salts, and invigorating herbs that your guests can use to embellish their own drinks. Being a good host or hostess doesn't mean that you must occupy yourself as bartender all evening. Remember, a gathering means group energy. Create a menu of cocktails for the evening. On large index cards, write the instructions for each drink and set it in a card holder. Have the ingredients, glasses, and embellishments by each index card. Encourage your guests to share in the creative process. You may need to lend a hand on their first try, but this will develop into an ice breaker and an enjoyable "party game" for everyone attending.

𝒇 Sour Mix

Using bottled water and freshly squeezed lemon juice will provide your cocktails with the best taste.

  1 cup sugar
  2 cups water
  2 cups fresh lemon juice

1. Combine sugar and water until all the sugar is dissolved. Add lemon juice and refrigerate.
2. Shake well before using. Store in refrigerator no longer than 5 days.

✟ Measurements and Equivalents

English Units

8 fluid ounces	equal	1 cup
2 cups	equal	1 pint
2 pints	equal	1 quart
4 quarts	equal	1 gallon

Approximate Conversions to Metric Measures from English Units

When You Know	Multiply By	To Find
fluid ounces	29.6	milliliters
cups	0.24	liters
pints	0.473	liters
quarts	0.946	liters
gallons	3.791	liters

Approximate Conversations to English Units from Metric Units

When You Know	Multiply By	To Find
milliliters	0.03	fluid ounces
liters	0.036	cubic feet
liters	2.1	pints
liters	1.06	quarts
liters	0.26	gallons

Approximate Conversions to Metric Measures from English Units

When You Know	Multiply By	To Find
ounces	28.3	grams
pounds	0.45	kilograms

Approximate Conversations to English Units from Metric Units

When You Know	Multiply By	To Find
grams	0.035	ounces
kilograms	2.2	pounds

Fahrenheit/Centigrade Conversion Table

TEMPERATURE

Formula:	Formula:
Degree C = $\dfrac{Degree\ F - 32}{1.8}$	Degree F = 1.8 x Degree C + 32

Acknowledgments

*T*HIS BOOK AND MY HAPPY LIFE are dedicated to my life partner, Chad Alan Olson. He has been a strong advocate of every dream, goal, insanity, harebrained idea, and success that I could conceive of. This time, however, the castle in the sky was a fulfillment of all my hopes, dreams, and desires recycled into this book. Chad has stood by me during both severe illness and exceptional health. When my mother passed away a short time ago, he was the person I took hold of when I had no mother to reassure me in my darkest moments.

To my grandmother, Thelma (Knutson) Anderson, thank you and I miss you. I have kept you alive these past thirty years by using everything you taught me and frequently speaking of all the goodness and comfort you gave me. It is almost as if you were back in Grand Forks living on Belmont Road. Only I haven't been home for a visit lately because I have been too busy.

To my mother, Judy Kay (Anderson) Lerma, I wish you were here to experience this. When I was about the age of ten, I enjoyed the butter cream frosting that you made from a recipe in your old Betty Crocker cookbook. I wanted to eat only the frosting and you wouldn't let me. One day, when you were working with Grandpa in the fields during the harvest, I brought your cookbook down from atop the refrigerator, found the recipe, and began what has been a long career of cooking and creating what I wanted to eat. I don't believe you comprehended it, but you set off a chain of events that has been very rewarding for me and many others. I never got to say good-bye or that I am sorry or how much I loved you. I inherited your stubborn streak, so I hope you understood who I was before you passed. I only hope that you are proud of me.

Many thanks go to my best friend, Daniel Paul Kenward, for coaching me to "put on a boa" when times got demanding. Your laughter and good nature have meant more to me than I will ever be able to articulate. For more years than we both care to verbalize, you have been my sunshine. You have been the reason I have bloomed all these years, and now I have created, in you, a fanatical gardener. I apologize, Ron; it's a lifetime malady.

To Dan's partner, Ronald Day Iverson—Wow!—and thank you for the extraordinary room design. I knew you were incredible, but I had no idea to what lengths you would go to make my book cover look so absolutely fabulous. One big drag queen kiss to you.

Many big hugs and kisses to Lorna Benson and Jeff Horwich for the use of their charming home and dining room. We arrived like a herd of well-dressed animals and overtook your home one evening. You've been nothing but encouraging, and you will always have my eternal gratitude. Salute!

More big hugs and kisses to Laura and Wyatt McCallum. Thank you, Wyatt, for wearing a red shirt on my book cover and being the most patient five-year-old boy anyone could ask to sit for several hours. Laura, thank you for being a friend and allowing all of us to be a part of the village in Wyatt's life. Gosh, it's been fun.

I don't know if the words in the English language exist to completely express my appreciation to my photographer and friend, Lanee' Benson and her assistant photographer and our friend, Jennifer Frederick Terrell. You both did such a fantastic job. You took a dazed subject and made him look not half bad. I will be eternally grateful for that the rest of my (and my book's) life. I am glad you've both been part of our garden.

Then there is Leslie Benson—"For you beautiful lady, anything!" Thank you for reading your journal of your travels through Spain and Portugal. Falling asleep in Venice in that fabulous hotel room under a Venetian painted ceiling while listening to your travels will be engraved forever in my mind. "Will you read us another story, Auntie Leslie?"

Linda Benson, thank you for having three magnificent girls who have become our family. Investigating exotic fruits on the island of Kauai at the fruit stand was wonderful, and I am so glad we have shared these moments. I hope you enjoy reading my book in your sunroom. I'll come down and join you in Decorah someday and share a glass of wine.

To our neighbors and good friends Mike and Mona Alf and their daughters Mollie and Chloe: this book and my success at the American Pie Festival would not have been possible without your family of taste testers. Some of my pies and foods may not have been remarkable, but you always accepted them with graciousness and offered sound opinions. Not only that, but our poor kitty would be a mess without your kindheartedness while we've been traveling. Thank you for being the sunshine in our east.

Many thanks must go all the way back to the late 1980s and early 1990s to two individuals that had so much to do with my outlook on life and instilling in me the love of the written word. Kathleen Hulley and Sheryl O'Donnell at the University of North Dakota were both instrumental in focusing a student who was flying in all directions. These two remarkable women are what the profession of teaching is all about. Even though it has been years since we have spoken or since I sat in your classrooms or office discussing writing, I still have the desire—and cannot remove from my head—the lessons of writing and exploration you both taught me. Thank you for providing me with a lifetime of desire to express myself.

Last, but more important and with great affection, my heartfelt admiration and gratitude for the friendship, conversations, and teaching by example how to be a good person at all times to Ursula Hovet of Thompson, North Dakota, and the University of North Dakota. How I miss our early-morning gab sessions in your office. I think of you often, and you will always be close to my heart for being such a dear woman. Thank you!

Index

To order additional copies of *Garden Country*:

Web: www.itascabooks.com

Phone: 1-800-901-3480

Fax: Copy and fill out the form below with credit card information.
         Fax to 763-398-0198.

Mail: Copy and fill out the form below. Mail with check or
         credit card information to:

         Syren Book Company
         5120 Cedar Lake Road
         Minneapolis, MN 55416

Order Form

Copies	Title / Author	Price	Totals
	Garden Country / **John Michael Lerma**	$15.95	$

Subtotal	$
7% sales tax (MN only)	$
Shipping and handling, first copy	$ 4.00
Shipping and handling, ___ add'l copies @$1.00 ea.	$
TOTAL TO REMIT	$

Payment Information:

__ Check Enclosed __ Visa/MasterCard		
Card number:	Expiration date:	
Name on card:		
Billing address:		
City:	State:	Zip:
Signature :	Date:	

Shipping Information:

__ Same as billing address __ Other (enter below)		
Name:		
Address:		
City:	State:	Zip: